The
Technical Manager

The Technical Manager

HOW TO MANAGE PEOPLE AND MAKE DECISIONS

Bruce F. Baird

Lifetime Learning Publications
Belmont, California
A division of Wadsworth, Inc.

London, Singapore, Sydney, Toronto, Mexico City

Jacket and Text Designer: Rick Chafian

Content Editor: Lorraine Anderson

Composition: Computer Typesetting Services, Inc.

Printed in the United States of America

2 3 4 5 6 7 8 9 10—87 86 85 84

Library of Congress Cataloging in Publication Data
Baird, Bruce F.
  The technical manager.
  Includes bibliographies and index.
  1. Industrial management. 2. Production management.
I. Title.
HD31.B323 1983   658.4   83-990
ISBN 0-534-97925-4

Contents

CONTENTS

Preface

Recent studies have shown that more than 75 percent of American engineers and scientists eventually hold technical management positions. Furthermore, managerial assignments tend to occur early in these individuals' careers and to occupy a major portion of the time spent in these careers. These scientists and engineers must have technical knowledge and skills concerning their particular field of technology. As technical managers, however, they need something more. They must also have the ability to convert their technical knowledge and that of their subordinates and peers into profitable results.

Technical managers must define objectives that coincide with the overall strategy of the organization, achieve results through the efforts of others, evaluate and control performance, motivate subordinates, make decisions in the presence of uncertainty, and, at the same time, manage their own careers. All too frequently, their formal technical training has not prepared them for these new responsibilities.

This book is for the engineer, scientist, or similar technical specialist with extensive training in a particular field who, because of this training and the judgment of a superior, is promoted into administration without being adequately prepared for it. The book presents a workable system of management that deals with results, delegation, feedback, control, and decision making. This system builds upon the strengths of the scientist or engineer and is based upon my observations and experiences as an engineer and an engineering manager.

Management concepts and specific steps for putting them into practice are presented here in a simple and clear format. I emphasize what a new technical manager must do to get off to a good start, to avoid being caught up in irrelevant activities, and to remain focused on high-priority results. The management approach I outline is practical (not theoretical) and has proved effective in real-world technical organizations.

I wish to express appreciation to all those managers who have contributed to my development as a manager, and to those others who have assisted in the preparation of this text. I especially wish to thank Lorraine Anderson, whose editorial and intellectual contributions have significantly improved the quality of presentation and content. Also, I am indebted to William Giegold, Bernard Sarchet, and Augustus Walker who read the original manuscript and offered valuable criticism.

Bruce F. Baird

The
Technical Manager

1.

Getting Off to a Good Start

It is not enough to have great qualities, we must also have the management of them.

LA ROCHEFOUCAULD

From this chapter you will learn:

- *Some characteristics you have as a scientist or engineer that will help you become a competent manager*
- *What characteristics are correlated with success in management*
- *What your primary purpose is as a manager, and how you can achieve it*
- *What you can do right now to get started*

Carl Hill earned a bachelor's degree in mechanical engineering at Rice University and a master's degree in the same discipline at M.I.T. He then accepted a position as systems engineer with a machinery manufacturing firm in California. He thoroughly enjoyed his work there. Even though he was often required to work through his lunch hour and into the evening, especially when contract deadlines approached, it gave him great satisfaction to solve knotty technical problems and, as he and his colleagues described it, "to advance the state of the art."

Then something happened. He was called into his boss's office and congratulated. Carl was to be the new engineering manager in charge of the entire project. The impact of this news didn't really hit home until the next week when he walked into his new office, sat in his new chair by his new desk, and stared at the wall for most of the morning. Over and over he thought to himself, "*What do I do? Where do I start?*"

Engineers and scientists are rarely trained for management

Carl's dilemma is typical. It happens daily. He had spent seven years in two outstanding institutions, was intelligent, and was superbly trained in his field of engineering. Unfortunately, he had not been required nor had he chosen to take a single course in management. Reliability and Energy Conversion had seemed more important at the time. Now he had to be concerned about the reliability of his subordinates and methods for converting their energy to accomplishment of project goals. The task was more challenging (and more frightening) than any engineering problem he had ever tackled.

Carl would admit that his promotion was not really a surprise. He had been working for it and thinking about it for years. But now he realized that he needed different competencies . . . of a managerial nature. He also knew that he had to maintain his technical competence at the same time. It was this double-barrelled challenge that bothered him. He wanted badly to be a successful manager but was not certain he had the necessary characteristics.

You are probably facing the same challenge and experiencing the same feelings as you read this book. You may be wondering if you have what it takes to manage. And you may be wondering how to approach your new assignment, in your first week, your first month, your first year of management. How should you deal with your subordinates? Your manager? What are the pitfalls you should avoid? How should you manage your own career?

Competence in management can be learned

Good managers are made, not born. You *can* develop competence in management, and the sole purpose of this book is to help you do so. In this chapter we'll look at the qualities you already possess that will help you become a good manager, others you can cultivate, and we'll introduce a first step you can take and a plan you can follow to achieve the primary goal of management.

2

You Already Have Some Traits of a Good Manager

Your scientific training has helped you develop several characteristics that competent administrators must have.

- You are *problem oriented.* Solving problems has been a major part of your technical training. It has also been a major thrust of your professional career. Advancing the state of the art requires solving problems. This is true of management, too, to some extent. A manager must be a problem solver, a problem recognizer, and, more importantly, a problem preventer. The difference is that you are no longer dealing with precise physical laws. Managers must make decisions in much less definitive situations involving human beings and uncertainty concerning the payoffs of courses of action. That is, managerial problems are usually less structured than technical problems.

Problem solving is important

- You are trained to be *scientific.* This translates to "unbiased, methodical, and rational." These are desirable characteristics for management.

- You are *comfortable with numbers* and quantitative approaches. Not everything in management can be reduced to a number; however, management information is most often numerical or quantitative in form. Your training in this respect will help you become a better decision maker.

Your unbiased, numerically-oriented skepticism is also important

- You are *skeptical.* You know that not everything is the way it seems to be at first glance. Why is that so? Why do we do things that way? Is there a better way? You will find out that in most organizations the person who knows *how* eventually ends up working for the person who knows *why.*

So you see that you already possess characteristics you can build on as a manager. You need not feel totally at sea as you begin your managerial career.

Five Other Traits Distinguish a Good Manager

What other characteristics should a manager have? Considerable research has shown that there is no single personal

3

characteristic which you *must* have in order to be a successful manager, without which you cannot be successful. Nonetheless, research *has* been able to isolate several characteristics that are highly correlated with managerial performance:

- *Intelligence.* This is a reasonable predictor of the probability of success up to a certain point. When very high levels of intelligence are reached, however, the reverse is true. Highly intelligent individuals may find a lack of abstract challenge in a management assignment.

- *Initiative.* This is a matter of initiating independent actions without outside stimulation and visualizing courses of action not apparent to others. Initiative becomes more important as one progresses from the operational level of management to top levels.

- *Self-confidence.* This is the inner feeling of self-assurance that one is performing effectively and dealing competently with problems in the organization.

- *Supervisory ability.* This is a complex ability to define assignments and direct the efforts of others toward the achievement of organizational objectives.

- *Goal orientation.* This is the constant directing of resources toward specific, well-defined goals.

The task ahead for you as an emerging manager is to utilize your high level of intelligence and scientific inclinations, orient yourself toward objectives, develop your ability to supervise others, and from positive experiences which result in successful performance build up your initiative and self-confidence.

Your Primary Purpose and Where to Start

The right traits will help you succeed as a manager only insofar as you apply them to achieving your primary purpose.

Your primary purpose is to establish an environment in which others are able to accomplish results that contribute to the overall mission of your organization.

4

Read that statement once again. It's important for you to understand at the outset that you are not the primary ball-carrier, the one who accomplishes most of the worthwhile results. Nor is your function to supervise in the classic sense of the term. As a manager of specialists your major functions are to challenge, guide, motivate, and achieve results. If you try to direct professionals closely, tell them what to do and how to do it, or visualize them as blue-collar workers with a degree, you will fail.

Your job is to help others do theirs

Begin now to familiarize yourself with your subordinates' backgrounds and qualifications. Start with personnel records. Review every page in every file. What is the educational background? Areas of specialization? Successes? Failures or gaps in training? Career plans or interests? What unique skills does each possess to contribute to the results your department is to accomplish? How may these skills be utilized most effectively?

Be objective at this stage. Do not assume these "partners" are all in the proper slots. Make notes and start a small file for each of these people. Anticipate that this initial source of information will be surprisingly inadequate — but it is a start. Plan to supplement these files frequently by adding information obtained through personal observation and face-to-face discussions with each individual.

If you have had difficulties with certain of these people in the past, try to put these conflicts aside. Your subordinates are now in a position to generate results that will make you look good, or conversely, increase your probability of failure. Similarly, you are in a position to provide challenge, meaningful assignments, and other rewards. This mutual dependence is something you must recognize from the outset. The best way for you to look good is for your subordinates to generate the proper results with support and encouragement from you.

A Plan for Achieving Your Primary Purpose

You can achieve your primary purpose by following this simple, coherent plan:

1. See yourself as a managerial system. Concentrate on output, making certain that its value exceeds the costs of inputs and activities.

2. Clarify what is expected of you and what you expect of your subordinates in terms of results.

Follow this plan to achieve results through others

3. Allow freedom of choice in methods used to achieve results.

4. Evaluate performance on the basis of output.

5. Provide frequent feedback. Design the system to generate feedback and encourage self-measurement and evaluation.

6. Reward contributions to the organization's objectives.

7. Help your subordinates grow personally and professionally.

The following chapters take up each element of this plan in detail, explaining why each is important and how to go about doing it. Later chapters help you understand your organization's structure, its strategy, and how to manage your own career.

Summary

- Scientists and engineers promoted to management are typically unprepared for their new assignment. You are not alone.
- Take stock of and acknowledge the characteristics you've developed that qualify you for management — your problem orientation, unbiased rationality, comfort with numbers, skepticism, and intelligence.
- Resolve to cultivate your initiative, self-confidence, supervisory ability, and goal orientation as you grow with the job.
- Recognize that your primary purpose as a manager is to enable others to achieve results.
- Begin now to familiarize yourself with your subordinates' capabilities.

2.

Managing for Results

Watch out when a man's work becomes more important than its objectives . . . when he disappears into his duties.

ALAN HARRINGTON

From this chapter you will learn:

- *Why it is useful to look at your organization, your department, and yourself as systems in terms of the black-box concept*
- *What your three basic options are for expending energy, and which you should choose to focus on*
- *What the activity trap is and how you can avoid it*
- *How to focus on results*

When I was promoted several years ago to a management position in a large organization, I inherited a subordinate who had been in his job for six years. He came to work early and left late. He brought his lunch in a brown bag so he could eat and get some work done during the lunch hour. He would turn off his office light for at least an hour every afternoon so it looked like he was gone, and move over to the window so he could work uninterrupted. He would see no one without an appointment and would run everywhere so as not to waste time in transit. I have never met anyone as busy, as dedicated to the organization, and as fanatical about managerial activities. After two years, I had to ask for his resignation because there was no output.

Fortunately for me, at the same time I inherited the activity fanatic, I also inherited the most competent manager I have ever known. He didn't come in early or leave late. As a matter of fact, he played nine holes of golf twice a week in the late afternoon. He would most often be found with his feet on his desk, relaxing with the *Wall Street Journal*. Memos from him were rare. "Why don't we" meetings (Why don't we do this? Why don't we try that?) were nonexistent in his department, yet his people were the most productive in the organization. He made management appear effortless. What was his secret?

He and his staff met from time to time to set objectives and tie them to goals of top management. These objectives were in terms of results . . . specific outputs . . . which were documented and distributed to the staff after they were agreed upon face to face. Each person knew precisely what was expected and by when. Informal meetings with each subordinate were held periodically to monitor progress toward achievement of the results. Every activity, every expenditure of resources, and every decision related in some way to achievement of a desired result. Each subordinate knew what he was responsible for achieving and the limits of his authority. Furthermore, all routine objectives were delegated to subordinates so that the boss had only to be concerned with setting strategy, monitoring progress, and dealing with exceptions to the routine. His staff was allowed great personal freedom to achieve results in their own way and they were committed to these objectives.

The contrast between these two managers couldn't have been greater. For the first, activity was what mattered; for the second, only results counted. In this chapter we'll consider why the second approach is so much more successful than the first. We'll start by looking at your organization as a system and will then consider the implications of this view for effective managerial behavior.

A Systems View of Your Organization

The concept of a "black box" is a familiar one to engineers. In college, engineering students are presented with a sealed box with terminals for input and output. The process going on inside the box is impossible to observe, but by manipulating input into the box and studying its output, students can learn something about the nature of the invisible process. Figure 2-1 illustrates the black-box concept.

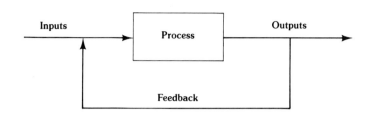

Figure 2-1. The black-box concept.

Inside the black box is a system — a collection of elements that are dependent and perform certain activities to produce outputs. An organization can be seen as a system. In this case, inputs to the system are resources necessary for operation, such as energy, matter, information, or money. The process is the transformation of input. It involves activities . . . things that are done. This process is usually complex. The transformation of inputs by the process generates outputs. These are the results of the combination of inputs and processes and, as such, are the purposes for existence of the system or organization.

Systems perform activities on inputs to produce outputs

An overriding principle of organizational systems is that the value of the output must justify the cost of the input and the processes.

Consider for a moment a typical manufacturing firm as a system. The input consists of people, capital, raw material, components, ideas, and so on. The process of stamping, machining, smelting, and so on transforms these inputs into finished products. Within the large system are a number of subsystems. The output of each subsystem becomes the input for another subsystem. The output of the production subsystem becomes the input for the distribution subsystem. Sales, research, accounting, and management are also subsystems. The interdependent nature of these subsystems is illustrated in Figure 2-2.

In an organizational system the output of each subsystem is crucial to the smooth functioning of the whole.

9

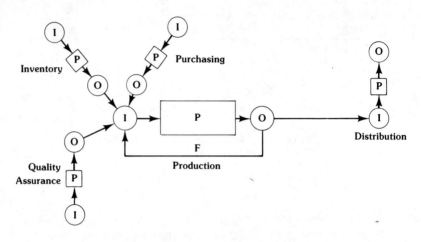

Figure 2-2. Some interdependent subsystems in a manufacturing organization.

So how does this discussion of black boxes, systems, and subsystems apply to you? The department you have been assigned to manage is like a black box. What goes on inside it is not important per se, but only in terms of its resulting output. The value of this output must justify the cost of the input and the process. And because your department is a subsystem, its output is crucial to the smooth functioning of your organization.

You are a managerial system

On another level, you can see *yourself* as a system, with three basic options for expenditure of your time and energy: you can choose to concentrate on inputs, activities, or outputs. We'll explore this idea next.

The Importance of Results

Pick up any book dealing with general training for managers and you will find a description of the functions of management, such as:

A manager creates conditions conducive to working, plans the work of subordinates, selects and trains them, directs and controls them, and evaluates their performance.

Frequent reference is made to coordinating, communicating, motivating, supervising, deputizing, and monitoring. What such a description neglects to mention is that it is possible to perform all these *activities* of management and stay very busy without generating a single useful *result*. The manager I had to fire had fallen into this trap.

Activities don't count . . . results do

Inputs, activities, or outputs: inevitably, one of these will become the focus of your energies as a manager. The proper focus is on output. Inputs and activities are important only insofar as they contribute to output.

A successful manager is one who gets the job done.

Admittedly, there are restraints that must often be considered. The ends do not always justify *any* means. The Committee to Reelect the President got the job done. Nixon was reelected. There are often moral, ethical, legal, emotional, and political constraints on your activities. You cannot run roughshod over people. Safety regulations that protect workers from exposure to personal danger must be obeyed. But within these constraints, output is the overriding criterion for competent management.

A corollary of this rule is that unless there is an effect upon results, the way a subordinate looks, his or her age, sex, religion, dress, and his or her activities should have no influence upon your evaluation or treatment of him or her. The only thing that counts is whether or not the job gets done!

Incompetent managers concentrate upon activity. Subordinates are evaluated in terms of what they do and how busy they are. The *truly* incompetent manager concentrates upon how people look while they perform the activity.

Looks don't count . . . results do

During a management conference, a supervisor in a large local hospital approached me during a coffee break. "I need some advice. I have a really serious management problem with a young man who works for me. We get along wonderfully and I really like him. He is the best housekeeper I have. He does thirty to thirty-five rooms every day, although the hospital standard is only seventeen.

11

The quality of his work is the best in the hospital. He works in the children's ward and tells them stories while he works. He cheers them up. He is incredibly clean. The jeans, white sweatshirt, and tennis shoes he wears are washed every day. His personal hygiene is just as good."

"Then what is the problem?" I asked.

"He has long hair and a beard," she replied, "and the hospital administrator is a retired Army colonel. The Colonel told me last week that he is not going to have a #$%& hippie in his hospital. 'Either get that clown to shave off the beard, cut the hair, and wear the white suit and shoes we provide or else fire him!!' "

I learned shortly afterward that the young man was indeed fired, and two people were hired to replace him. Learn from this example of incompetent management. The thing that truly counts is results!

The Activity Trap and How to Recognize It

Many managers become so involved with doing things right that they no longer do the right things. The activities that started out to transform inputs into outputs become ends in themselves rather than means. George Odiorne, a well-known management author and educator, calls this managerial problem the activity trap.[1] Your organization may already be caught in this trap. Its most common characteristics are these:

Characteristics of an organization in the activity trap

- *Considerable time is spent in meetings.* Most of these are "Why don't we" sessions. Why don't we do this? Why don't we try that? Why don't we wait until Tuesday when we will have more information? Why don't we have another meeting tomorrow?

- *Decisions are made by groups.* No single person makes critical choices and, hence, no single manager may be held responsible if the decision turns out to be incorrect.

- *Great paperwork is generated.* The secretaries are busy. The file clerks are busy. The mail room is busy. The memos fly and the initial reaction of any outsider is "Wow! These people are really getting after it!"

- *Morale is low and turnover is high.* Many workers spend company time redoing resumes, reading want ads in journals and newspapers, and complaining about the incompetence of the bosses.
- *Objectives are unclear.* If you ask the purpose of the activities, the usual response is "Don't ask me where I am going. I am too busy getting there to discuss it right now."
- *Workers are not certain of what the boss expects* so they depend upon busywork in the hope that they'll do something that is pleasing to the boss.
- The only *feedback* workers receive is *once a year* in the annual performance review, so the rest of the year they wonder how they are doing and figure if they look busy the boss will be impressed.

Recall that the competent manager I described at the beginning of this chapter avoided all these pitfalls. To start with, he and his subordinates had specific objectives in terms of results. He knew what outputs were expected of his department, and his subordinates knew specifically how they were each to contribute to those outputs. You must follow this example if you are to avoid the activity trap.

Know Your Department's Mission

Before another day goes by, clarify key aspects of your assignment with your boss. Do this face-to-face. Concentrate upon a few critical questions:

- What are the unique contributions of your group? The major reasons for its existence? Its place in the mission of the larger organization? If it didn't exist, what worthwhile output would be lost?
- What specific results are expected by your boss? How are these measured or described?
- What are the priorities? Which results are critical? If resources must be redirected, which results may be minimized or ignored?

Clarify the results your boss expects

- By what point in time should the output be available?
- What is the nature of your authority? Its limitations? What kinds of decisions are yours?

- How often does your boss wish to have progress reviews? Be sure to set a date for the next one.
- What is your superior's evaluation of the current efficiency and effectiveness of your department? What are its major strengths? Weaknesses? Does he or she have suggestions for major areas of improvement?
- What specific commitments will he or she make to help you learn so you may grow in the job?

Follow up this meeting with a written statement of the answers to these questions. If you still have uncertainties, go see your boss. Do not make any unwarranted assumptions. Clarification now will avoid major conflicts later. Do not get caught in the "But I thought you said . . ." trap!

Your next step is a meeting of you and your immediate subordinates to clarify and agree upon your department's mission. Prepare and distribute a written statement of the major conclusions reached in your meeting with your boss. Specific results, priorities, schedules, and commitments should be discussed openly. Encourage frankness as you consider the following:

- Where are the pitfalls?
- Are the expected results reasonable but challenging?
- Are the scheduled milestones achievable?
- What immediate input and/or support do they need from you for an initial analysis of the program?

Outline your managerial plan (from Chapter 1) and try to demonstrate by your actions that you believe it and will operate in terms of it. Give your subordinates an appropriate time period to think about the major points raised in this meeting. Listen carefully to their comments, realizing that this session is for both information-getting as well as information-giving. Remember that no one learns anything while talking. Close the meeting with a specific plan of action.

Next, you should schedule one-on-one meetings with each individual. The importance of these meetings and how to go about them is the topic of the next chapter.

Summary

- Think of your organization and your department as complex systems of activity converting inputs into outputs.

- The organization exists to produce outputs, not to perform activities. The same holds true for your department and for you. Results are what count.

- Capable managers clarify what they expect in terms of output from their subordinates and then evaluate performance in terms of achievement of these results.

- Incompetent, ineffective managers concentrate their energies on input and activity. Truly incompetent managers emphasize appearance.

- Organizations and managers caught in the activity trap have forgotten their objectives and become absorbed in duties and functions. You must avoid this trap if your managerial career is to be successful.

- Begin right now to clarify the output your boss wants from you and you want from your subordinates. Resolve to manage for results.

Note

1. G. S. Odiorne, *Management and the Activity Trap* (New York: Harper & Row, 1974). This well-done work outlines reasons for the trap, the end of motivation, and the causes for people shrinking in their work. It ends with some observations on how to create an environment that will help people grow.

Further Readings

1. A good collection of articles dealing with systems and their environments is F. E. Emery (editor), *Systems Thinking* (Baltimore: Penguin Books, 1974).

2. For a more detailed discussion of engineering systems analysis, see R. de Neufville and J. H. Stafford, *Systems Analysis for*

Engineers and Managers (New York: McGraw-Hill, 1971). This work outlines modern concepts of systems design with an emphasis on a blend of mathematical and economics models.

3. Another competent introduction to systems thinking from a managerial point of view is P. P. Schoderbek, A. G. Kefalas, and C. G. Schoderbek, *Management Systems: Conceptual Considerations* (Dallas: Business Publications Inc., 1975).

3.

Agreeing on Objectives

As to us—we are uncertain people, who are chased by the spirits of our destiny from purpose to purpose, like clouds by the wind.

PERCY SHELLEY

From this chapter you will learn:

- *Why it is important for subordinates to know what is expected*
- *How objectives should be worded, and what areas they should cover*
- *How you can set objectives for situations where results are hard to measure*
- *How you should approach agreeing on objectives to gain the maximum commitment from your subordinates*

One of my colleagues was retained by a large research organization in the Northwest. She was to analyze and recommend improvements in their management practices and policies. After a full day of interviews with middle and top managers she retired to the company cafeteria to go over her notes and check the completeness of her information. Fred, one of the second-level managers she had interviewed, sat down and asked if he could see the notes she had taken with his boss. She was hesitant to do this even though the boss had not stated that their discussion was confidential. It seemed highly unethical to her to relate the details of Fred's lack of performance and his boss's expectations and evaluation. When she hesitated, Fred became very emotional and explained that he had a sick child and heavy debts, the unemployment rate in the area was eighteen percent, he had had two poor annual performance ratings in the last two years, and he was certain he would be fired if the next rating was as bad as the last two. She was very moved by Fred's pleas but still felt she could not hand over the notes, so she said, "I am going to get a cup of coffee. If you look at the bottom sheets in that right-hand stack while I am gone, I cannot stop you. But I cannot show them to you." When she returned in a few minutes Fred was gone.

A serious problem many subordinates must live with . . . what does the boss expect?

Several months later, she received a long distance call from the boss. He said, "Dr. Jones, I don't know what you did with one of my subordinates when you were here, but I would like to negotiate a fee with you and have you return and do the same thing with all of my people. His performance has improved so much I cannot believe he is the same person."

"Which subordinate?" asked Jones.

"Fred Williams."

She somewhat uneasily told the boss about Fred's visit to the cafeteria and her trip to get a cup of coffee. There was a long silence and the boss finally said, "You mean Fred saw the list of things I told you I expect him to produce?"

"Yes, sir, he did."

After another long silence, the boss said very slowly, "That sonuvabitch cheated!!!"

This story is absolutely true. Admittedly, the case is extreme, but it is not uncommon. There are lots of Freds in corporations, hospitals, government agencies, and scientific organizations, wondering what their bosses expect of them. The importance of avoiding this expectations gap is discussed in this chapter; so is the proper method of setting objectives and gaining commitment to these objectives from your subordinates.

Subordinates Need to Know Your Expectations

From Fred's story it should be clear that a lack of knowledge of the boss's expectations can be devastating to a subordinate's morale and performance. George Odiorne compares this situation to a runner's competing in a race of unknown length. "Am I in a 100-yard dash, a mile run, or the Boston Marathon?" Perhaps the race is a hurdle race, and the subordinate is blindfolded. "Run!" says the boss. "And jump when you come to a hurdle." Most likely the subordinate bounds down the track jumping at the wrong times and looking very silly. Every once in a while he correctly perceives a hurdle and jumps at precisely the right time but catches his toe on the top and lands astride it. "I forgot to tell you," says the boss, "I raised it six inches last week."

How can you perform in a contest whose objective is unknown?

This style of management can drive a worker right into the activity trap. When specific results haven't been agreed upon by superior and subordinate, the subordinate covers his anatomy with busyness. He or she wastes a major part of the working day trying to guess what the boss really wants. And lack of agreement on results can cause other management problems. How can you judge performance if it is never thoroughly defined? How can you deal out rewards without a clear statement of what results are to be rewarded? How can your people grow professionally when the criterion of growth keeps shifting?

Despite these harmful effects of the expectations gap, research has shown that it is pervasive. Hundreds of superior/subordinate pairs have been interviewed and their answers to these two questions compared:

- What are the subordinate's major areas of responsibility?
- What specific results does the boss expect?

Their answers usually are not the same. Where *routine* responsibilities are discussed, the boss and subordinate usually do not agree on about 25 percent of them . . . and these are the easy ones to agree upon. On *problem-solving* responsibilities the lack of agreement increases to 50 percent. On creative or *innovative* responsibilities, attempts to improve the overall nature of the organization, disagreement averages 90 percent.[1]

The expectations gap is real

> *Most subordinates do not have a clearly defined agreement with their boss about specific results to be produced.*

The other side of this coin, as we learned from Fred, is that when a subordinate knows exactly what is expected of him or her in

19

terms of output and becomes committed to it, that person's performance is likely to be top-notch. When you spend time face-to-face with your subordinates and agree upon specific results, you gain several advantages:

- *You free yourself of detail.* When your subordinates have a specific destination, constant direction and supervision are not required of you. You can use the exception principle. The subordinate knows what is expected, and as long as the results are being achieved, there is no reason to bother you. Minor deviations can be discussed during regularly scheduled periodic reviews as time passes. When results are not forthcoming, then the subordinate can involve you. You will then learn of the "exception" and can take it into account as something to be dealt with and, if possible, resolved.

- *What you want to achieve becomes clearer in your own mind.* You are challenged and forced to think hard about whether your objectives are valid or whether they are false goals adopted because they are easy to measure.

- *You gain your subordinates' commitment.* It has been well established in numerous studies that people are more committed to achieving objectives they have helped define. You will find that the simple process of involving your subordinates directly in the determination of the objective and the level of attainment which is to be achieved will significantly improve the chance of reaching the desired result. This is partially because they understand the nature of the objective and accept it. But it is more than that. They become committed personally to achieving a result by a particular point in time because they participated in its birth. This involvement/commitment idea is crucial for success.

Now that you understand why agreeing upon expectations is so important for you and your subordinates, let's look at the details of how to formulate specific objectives.

Objectives Should Be Specific

Good management starts with clear objectives. What exactly is a clear objective? It's a result that is specific, well defined, observable, and verifiable.

Many corporations have a set of written objectives that sound like motherhood and an early spring. They include goals such as fair prices, sound wages, high return on investment, and good community relations. These not only conflict with each other, but they are most often so vague that it is not possible to tell whether or not they have been achieved. This problem also exists with individual departments and managers.

You can't get the job done if it is not defined in terms of specific results

When I was appointed the director of new product development in a medium-sized chemical company, the director of research and development proudly presented me with a statement of the objectives of my new position: *Within three years generate five million dollars worth of new business without significant investment of capital.* What does the five million refer to? Sales or profits? Is this an annual figure or what is to be generated during all three years? What are new products? Is a new use for an existing product included? A new customer? What is a significant investment? $10,000 or $200,000? If you want five million in new product business, can you possibly achieve the objective without "significant" investment?

> *A properly constructed objective defines a destination, not an activity or a direction. It is a tangible result that signals the termination of activity or the revision of it because the destination has now been reached.*

As another example, consider a research project undertaken some years ago by a Western chemical company. Phthalocyanine Blue is a fragile organic dye. An engineer felt that a proper vehicle combined with additives to stabilize the Phthalocyanine Blue molecules could result in a superior high temperature lubricant. The problem was twofold: What vehicle and additives were appropriate, and what combination of pressure and temperature would be optimal for high volume production? She submitted the following objective to her boss as the basis for funding of the initial study dealing with construction of a pilot plant:

> To investigate the feasibility of establishing a pilot plant in the Martinez facility for the production of Phthalocyanine Blue High Temperature Lubricant.

Assume you are her boss. What would you tell her about this objective?

**Never allow
activities as
objectives . . .
and be specific**

First of all, *investigate* and *establish* are activities, not results. Are you willing to pay for activities? Where is the result? If you sign off on the study, what is the output? Is the study written or oral? What will it contain? By when? If you approve it in its present configuration, you will likely get some unpleasant surprises when the feasibility study is completed.

Instead, suppose the objective is rewritten as:

> By July 1, 198_, a written report will be submitted to the Capital Expenditures Committee concerning the feasibility of constructing a pilot plant for the production of Phthalocyanine Blue Lubricant. The report will cover, as a minimum: cost estimates, construction time, safety considerations, specific benefits derived, analysis of cost/time/volume/quality tradeoffs, and recommended action.

The result is now defined specifically. Not only will you feel more comfortable about the project but, if she is capable, so will your subordinate.

A third example illustrates how having a well-defined objective is essential to determining whether to terminate or revise activity. During World War II a large number of British merchant ships were seriously damaged or sunk by enemy aircraft attacks in the Mediterranean. The obvious countermeasure was to equip the vessels with antiaircraft equipment and crews. Because of the expense involved and because antiaircraft equipment was in great demand elsewhere, not all ships were so modified. On those that were modified, the crews were trained in short periods of time with little opportunity to develop great proficiency, and consequently very few enemy aircraft were shot down by the merchant fleet. This led to demands from some quarters to remove the crews and equipment for other more efficient assignments. The British high command decided to remove them based upon the percentage of attacking enemy aircraft shot down, a rather obvious measure of effectiveness of antiaircraft weapons.

**Be certain
your objective
is what you
really want to
accomplish**

Before the action was taken, however, operational data were analyzed to settle the question of alternative uses of scarce resources. The data showed that only 4 percent of the attacks resulted in an enemy aircraft being shot down, a very poor result compared with those of other possible applications of identical

22

equipment and crews. On the other hand, it became obvious that planes shot down was *not* the proper criterion. The equipment and crews were put on the ship to *protect the ship,* not shoot down enemy aircraft. With this objective in mind, the proper measure of effectiveness would be whether the ship was less likely to be damaged or sunk if it had the equipment than if it had no anti-aircraft equipment. Did the antiaircraft fire sufficiently affect the accuracy of the plane's attack so that the chance of serious damage to the ship was reduced?

In fact, the data showed that regardless of the relative inaccuracy of the fire and despite the low proportion of planes shot down, the chance of a ship's surviving was more than doubled by the presence of antiaircraft equipment and crews. Once the proper objective was recognized (saving ships rather than shooting down planes), the results could easily be seen to merit the effort, and the high command left the equipment and crews intact.

Objectives Should Cover Every Key Area of Concern

Every manager must be concerned with the four key areas of *volume, quality, cost,* and *maintenance.* Volume might deal with units produced, cases sold, projects completed, new products developed, or contracts signed. Quality deals with distinctive properties or character of output in terms of merit or superiority. Cost deals with resources consumed. Maintenance involves preserving in some existing state of efficiency both physical and human assets.

The four major concerns for management

Setting objectives in these key areas often involves making tradeoffs. The areas of volume, quality, and cost are often at odds. It is possible to maximize volume by ignoring quality and/or cost. Quality can be maximized by minimizing volume and ignoring cost. Cost can be minimized by producing zero volume. In order to be successful as a manager, you must achieve proper levels of volume with acceptable levels of quality for minimum cost. Just exactly what constitutes "proper" levels of volume, "acceptable" levels of quality, and "minimum" cost is something you must agree upon with your boss. Then you are in a position to translate these desired results into specific objectives for your subordinates.

As you consider the results you want your subordinates to achieve, ask yourself these questions:

- Within each of these key areas, what specifically can be observed to assess performance?
- What specific ratios, percentages, or other measures will tell me whether or not the key area is under control at appropriate levels of output?
- For aspects of the job that are difficult to measure, how will I know when the job is well done?

These measures of performance are called *indicators* and, ideally, they are specific, quantifiable, or describable, and in terms of results rather than activities.

The most useful indicators are those that will highlight problems while there is still time to take corrective action (for example, "quality of incoming raw materials"). These leading indicators are "watch out's." Indicators that will highlight problems only after it is too late to take preventive action are important but not as helpful (for example, "customer complaints" or "turnover of high potential employees"). These lagging indicators are "gotcha's." Table 3-1 shows some suggested indicators of performance in each of the four key areas, and also in the areas of profitability and productivity, areas of concern to higher levels of management.

Objectives Should Include a Range of Values

Assume one of your responsibilities is the production of some durable good, say, a small electrical appliance. You and your boss have agreed that the target level of production is eighty units a day. Suppose production during a particular week has averaged seventy-eight units a day. Are you in trouble? The issue, of course, is whether or not seventy-eight is significantly different from eighty. Alternatively, suppose output has averaged eighty-one per day. Is this performance truly exceptional and significantly better than the standard of eighty?

Single values are not sufficient

Once you think carefully about these questions you will realize they are unanswerable, for both your boss and you. "I fell two units short each day this week! I wonder how the boss will feel about that?" Or "I achieved her standard and one more unit besides. I

Table 3-1. Some Suggested Indicators of Performance in Key Areas.

Area of Results to Be Achieved	Indicator of Performance
Quality	Raw material % defective No. of customer complaints Internal reject % No. and cost of billing errors Cost of spoiled work Warranty costs
Volume	No. of units produced Sales $ per period No. of calls per day No. of projects completed on time
Cost	Actual to standard, by product Travel expenses Worker's compensation cost Direct/indirect labor ratio Overall + or − budget No. and value of cost-reducing ideas
Maintenance	Downtime of equipment $ spent in preventive maintenance No. of training programs completed No. of promotable persons Courses completed successfully Job enrichment plans formulated
Profitability	Return on investment Profit as a % of sales $ profit per product line Cash flow
Productivity	$ cost per unit Units produced per worker hour Downtime of equipment Actual/standard cost ratio, by product

hope she decides that is fantastic!" All this uncertainty is unnecessary if you follow a simple but important principle:

Objectives should always be expressed in terms of three levels — minimum, expected, and maximum output.

To determine what exactly these levels should be, ask yourself these questions:

- What is a *realistic* target, performance that will occur if things go as expected? If resources, labor, equipment, and other factors of production are managed adequately, what level of output is most likely?
- If raw materials are of high quality and always available, breakdowns are infrequent, and productivity increases, what is the best possible output you can expect, within reason?
- If for various reasons production falls behind the expected target level, what will be the minimum tolerable output?

You can conceptualize these three levels of achievement as shown in Figure 3-1.

Once your subordinates know all three levels, much of the uncertainty has been removed from their recurring duties. Furthermore, as long as the process is in control you can use the exception principle and concentrate your energies on other aspects of your job. Your subordinates know the target, the ceiling, and the floor. Only when production drops below the floor do they need to come

A range reduces uncertainty

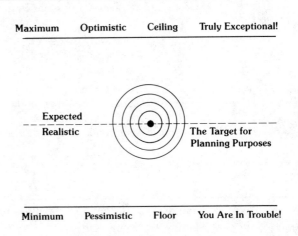

Maximum   Optimistic   Ceiling   Truly Exceptional!

Expected
Realistic   The Target for Planning Purposes

Minimum   Pessimistic   Floor   You Are In Trouble!

Figure 3-1. Every objective should specify a range of values.

and bother you. When production exceeds the ceiling, they know they can expect to be rewarded.

One caution. You must take care to agree to an optimistic level that is possible under some achievable set of conditions. If this level is set too high, motivation and incentive will be destroyed. "There is no way I can achieve that level, so why even try?" Similarly, pessimistic performance must be set at a level that still leaves the process with some hope of recovery, that is, a level that is not fatal.

Note also that there is no reason for the floor and ceiling to be symmetrical relative to the realistic level. The magnitude of the differences between realistic and pessimistic and between realistic and optimistic will be a function of the process, its variability, the cost associated with underachieving, the benefits of optimistic output, and to some extent the relative bargaining skills of you and your subordinates.

Setting Objectives When Results Are Hard to Measure

One successful manager once said to me, "If you can't count it, measure it, describe it, or verbalize it, you probably do not know what you want and ought to forget it as an objective!" But many of the tasks engineers and scientists do are ill-structured and seemingly unmeasurable. How do you define objectives when results are intangible? Doing so is difficult and creativity is required, but there *is* a method you can use.

First, think about what you hope to *make happen*. Decide on five or six critical indicators in your key areas of concern. For instance, indicators might be in the areas of customer relations, cost controls, staff and self-development, completion of projects within schedule, research proposals submitted, etc.

For these critical few indicators, the most reliable measures are real data based on physical objects that may be involved (number of items produced, dollar volume of sales, barrels of product manufactured, etc.). When raw data cannot be used, an index or ratio is the next best indicator (a percentage, a fraction, etc.). If neither of the above is appropriate, try using a scale such as "Rated from 1 to 10" or "Excellent, Good, Fair, Poor, Unacceptable." Some arbitrary descriptor such as "Better than" or "Worse than" might be used.

Measures can range from quantitative to verbal

27

General verbal descriptions of results to be achieved are the least desirable but still have usefulness and may be the only thing possible when tasks are very hard to measure.

When you have decided how your indicators are to be described, you should arrive at descriptions of optimistic, realistic, and pessimistic levels of performance for each. Then weight the indicators so that the relative order of their importance is clear to your subordinates.

The following example illustrates the process. Suppose one of your subordinates is a technical service manager. You agree that in her key areas of concern, the critical indicators are special orders, cost estimates, projects, production estimates, and customer complaints. You verbally describe optimistic, realistic, and pessimistic levels of performance for each of these indicators. Table 3-2 shows the results you agree on.

If useful, fourth and fifth levels could be specified between best and expected and between expected and worst. The indicators could be weighted in terms of relative importance; for example, special orders might be the most important of the five and thus weighted most heavily. When you have set specific objectives like these, it will be easy for you to check your subordinate's progress from time to time against her commitment.

The Right Approach to Agreeing on Objectives

Now that you understand the importance of objectives and how to go about defining them, you're ready to meet one-on-one with your subordinates. Since you are new to management, these sessions should provide you with an opportunity to learn about the current status of the individual as well as to agree on objectives for the future. The following guidelines should help you maximize your chance of gaining commitment from your subordinates for the production of output.

Clarification of objectives must be face-to-face

First, *discuss your subordinates' key areas of responsibility and measures of evaluation face-to-face.* Do not ever attempt to reach agreement through the mail. It is difficult enough to agree during a personal discussion. It is impossible to reach an agreement with memos. Even if a subordinate's work station is separated from

Table 3-2. Setting Objectives for a Technical Service Manager.

OBJECTIVE INDICATORS

ATTAINMENT LEVELS	Special Orders	Cost Estimates	Projects	Production Estimates	Customer Complaints
OPTIMISTIC Best Anticipated Outcome	95 percent of special orders designed and engineered within eight working days.	Actual production costs are within 5 percent of cost estimates on every project.	Three projects are formally incorporated in company's long range plan.	90 percent of production estimates for special sales inquiries completed within 48 hours of receipt and none take more than 72 hours.	No formal customer complaints.
REALISTIC Expected Level of Success	90 percent of special orders designed and engineered within eight working days.	Actual production costs are within 5 percent of cost estimates on 90 percent of projects and no estimate is off by more than 20 percent.	One or two projects are formally incorporated in company's long range plan.	80 percent of production estimates for special sales inquiries completed within 48 hours of receipt and none take more than 72 hours.	One to three formal customer complaints.
PESSIMISTIC Worst Anticipated Outcome	80 percent of special orders designed and engineered within eight working days.	Actual production costs are within 5 percent of cost estimates on 80 percent of projects and no more than two are off by more than 20 percent.	No projects are formally incorporated in company's long range plan.	70 percent of production estimates for special sales inquiries completed within 48 hours of receipt and none take more than 72 hours.	More than three formal customer complaints.

yours by many miles, the discussion of objectives must be a personal one, face-to-face, eyeball-to-eyeball. There is no more productive way you can spend your time than this. Minutes or hours spent clarifying expectations will free days and weeks for you later on.

Second, *both you and your subordinates must do your homework before this discussion.* Your subordinate must have some idea of answers to the following questions:

- How do I view my current work assignment?
- Are my responsibilities and authority clear?
- Is the information in the boss's file up to date? Are there skills unknown to the boss?
- What commitment will I make to achieve key results by some specific point in time?
- What are my key areas of responsibility?
- What are some indicators that would be appropriate for evaluation of results?
- What are the standards for my job?
- What obstacles do I anticipate? How can the boss help remove these?
- What resources and help do I need from the boss so I can honor my commitments?
- What innovations or problem-solving objectives interest me?
- Do I have a plan for my career?

You should also have a basic notion of answers to these same questions. You should insist upon realistic levels of achievement, levels that have a reasonable probability of attainment, levels that will stretch but not break the subordinate. This is a very fine line and it may take many years for you to develop a feeling for it. If the goals are set too low, the subordinate will underachieve and fail to grow. Moreover, your department will not reach levels of output that might otherwise be attained. On the other hand, if you insist upon levels that are unrealistically high, the subordinate's commitment will be lost immediately. "There is no way I can possibly reach that level, regardless of what I do, so why should I even try?" All of these issues should be thought out *before* the meeting takes place.

Third, *the process must be one of negotiation.* You cannot present a set of objectives and tell your subordinate "This is what you will achieve!" unless there is no other alternative. Mandated results will not gain commitment from engineers or scientists. Any serious disagreement about either the key areas of responsibility or the level of achievement should be brought out in the open and discussed honestly. Even if this causes conflict, it is much better to get it out on the table *now* and resolve it than to wait until later and find out when the annual performance review takes place that the subordinate has sabotaged some portion of the job.

Commitment requires negotiation

Fourth, *the subordinate should have a chance to present his or her entire package of potential objectives without criticism or in-depth discussion of any single objective.* When this package has been defined for you, *then* you can ask questions such as "Why is this important?" "How did you arrive at this level?" "What would be the consequences of ignoring this and perhaps substituting that?"

A common question at this point is "What if my subordinates want to set objectives that are too low?" In this case, you should state explicitly that the results are too unambitious and you must be prepared to justify this conclusion in terms of specific evidence. Surprisingly, the reverse situation is more often true. Numerous sales executives have told me a major problem is subordinates who want to set objectives too *high*. Later, with the realization that the result is not achievable, the subordinate loses commitment. I suspect this overzealousness may also be true for many technical subordinates. The superior's problem is then one of convincing the scientist/engineer that he should not commit himself to producing so much in such a short time. Think through with him or her what has to be done, by whom, by when, the probability of success on the first try, etc. Is this result humanly possible?

Last, *the agreement must be documented.* One of the parties should agree to write down the key areas, the indicators of performance, and the levels to be achieved by some particular point in time. Each of you should have a copy of this documentation. Which person generates the documentation is unimportant. The critical things to be kept in mind are that the documentation must be done immediately after the dialog takes place and both parties must have a written copy of the agreement. If the person who does not write the agreement questions whether the written version is accurate, then another dialog must take place, face-to-face, until documented agreement is achieved.

Document the agreement and each keep a copy

The ultimate objective of this entire process is *commitment.* A dictionary definition of this term would probably use words such as *trust* and *take charge of.* This is precisely what I am suggesting. The boss is saying, "Let's define the results you are to achieve so you can take charge of these responsibilities. I do not wish to be concerned with the minor details unless we are talking about a detail that could threaten the entire project. I trust you as a competent human being. If you are willing to commit yourself to achieving these results by this point in time, I will commit myself to support you in any way I can. And I promise not to change any of this agreement without first talking personally with you about it."

In summary,

Commitment for results will have a maximum chance of being achieved if negotiated openly and honestly, documented, and defined in realistic but challenging levels for a specific period of time.

Summary

- Agreeing on objectives with your subordinates can free you from detail, help you clarify what you hope to achieve, and gain your subordinates' commitment. Not agreeing can devastate morale and productivity.
- Set objectives that are specific, that cover the key areas of volume, cost, quality, and maintenance, and that allow for a range from pessimistic to realistic to optimistic.
- To set objectives when results are intangible, verbalize what you hope to make happen in key areas of responsibility.
- Gain commitment to objectives from your subordinates by sitting down with each face-to-face, giving prior thought to key questions, being open to negotiation, hearing out the subordinate's ideas, and documenting the agreement.

Note

1. The numerical values are from G. S. Odiorne, *Management and the Activity Trap* (New York: Harper and Row, 1974), p. 28.

Further Readings

1. For lucid treatments of setting objectives, see R. L. Morasky, "Defining Goals — A Systems Approach," *Long Range Planning* (Vol. 10; April 1977), p. 85, and R. A. Webber, *Management: Basic Elements of Managing Organizations* (Homewood, Ill.: Richard D. Irwin, 1979), Ch. 8, "Planning Objectives and Goals."

2. If you are interested in a more general treatment of the stresses involved in actual boss/subordinate relationships, read D. L. Woods, *My Job, My Boss and Me* (Belmont, Calif.: Lifetime Learning Publications, 1980).

4.

Delegating Authority

When a manager realizes he can call others in to help him do a job better than he can do it alone, he has taken a big step in his life.

ANDREW CARNEGIE

From this chapter you will learn:

- *Why delegation is important to your success as a manager*
- *Why many managers find it difficult to delegate*
- *What the proper approach is to delegation*

Once you and your subordinates have agreed upon objectives, you must be willing to trust the subordinates and allow them some personal freedom in the methods they use to accomplish results. You must also entrust some of your authority to them. This is the process of delegation.

Without delegation, there would be no need for a managerial organization. One person would retain all authority and make all decisions. Clearly, as the organization grows this becomes impossible and the overworked manager finds it necessary to allow someone to assist him or her. Researchers have concluded that one of the major reasons businesses fail is inability of key managers to delegate, thus continuing a centralization of authority as the organization grows in size and becomes more complex.

Delegation is also a very effective way of helping your subordinates grow. Giving them a piece of your job motivates increased

*Delegation is
essential to the
growth of your
organization
and your
subordinates*

productivity and job satisfaction. It stretches the subordinate and forces him or her to develop new skills. It removes some of the burden from you, thus allowing you to concentrate on more important objectives. Unfortunately, it is also one of the most difficult lessons for many managers to learn. In this chapter we will explore why that is. We will also look at the difference between delegating authority and responsibility, different styles and levels of delegation, and some guidelines to help you delegate effectively.

You Can Delegate Authority but Not Responsibility

One of the cornerstones of management theory is that you can delegate authority but not responsibility. You may assign a task to a subordinate and delegate the authority for a decision to him. You can hold him responsible for successful accomplishment, but if he makes an error and is unsuccessful, *you* are still responsible.

The authority can be given away, but you cannot divest yourself of the responsibility.

For example, suppose your teenage son wishes to purchase an automobile and asks you to cosign a note at the bank. You do so and tell him, "You may buy the car, but you must take care of it and you must make the loan payments." However, if he misses some payments, who does the bank hold responsible? You, of course.

There are exceptions to this above principle, but they are rare. A number of executives were convicted of price fixing by a federal court several years ago, but the presidents of the large electrical equipment companies that employed these executives were *not* convicted. They argued that their organizations were so large and complex that they could not possibly know everything that was going on in every department. Because there was no direct evidence to implicate them, they were acquitted, although technically they could have been held responsible for the deeds of their subordinates.

Why Many Administrators Cannot Delegate Effectively

Managers who cannot delegate effectively usually complain about being overworked (and they probably *are*), but they are uncomfortable letting someone else do some of the work. This discomfort may exist for a number of reasons:

- *"I can do it better."* Some managers feel they can handle the activity or make the decision better than a subordinate. They lack confidence in that person, and so they refuse to let go of any authority. At the other extreme, some managers lack self-confidence, and so they refuse to delegate because they are afraid the subordinate will do the job *better* than they can and thus show them up.

- *"Delegation takes too much time."* The manager feels that briefing the subordinate, monitoring performance, and following up on final results will consume more time than doing the job herself.

- *The manager lacks the proper skills for delegation.* Certain rules must be followed in delegating properly. If a manager does not know these rules and cannot communicate and plan effectively, delegation will not work and the manager will be reluctant to attempt it . . . or to reattempt it because it didn't work last time.

- *The employee may resist the assumption of more authority.* He may lack self-confidence or may be fearful of what will happen to him if something goes wrong.

- *The control mechanism may be improperly designed.* Delegation requires a system for monitoring performance and providing feedback for both the subordinate and the boss. If this system does not exist or is ineffective, the boss will be reluctant to delegate because he may lose control of the situation.

Attitudes and problems that can keep a manager from delegating

You Can Delegate to Different Degrees

There is no single form of delegation. Many different shades exist and every manager must choose which one operates best for him or her in a given situation. At one extreme is the most anemic form. "Investigate this issue. Get the facts for me. Take no action. I will make the decision." At the other extreme is, "You make the decision and take whatever action is appropriate. No further discussion with me is necessary." Between these extreme positions there are various gradations of delegated authority, such as:

- Let me know what our options are. What are the advantages and disadvantages of each? I will make the decision.

You can retain or give away as much authority as you want

- Investigate the problem and recommend a decision along with your reasons for choosing this alternative. I will then review your recommendation and make the decision.

- You decide what to do but do not take any action until we have discussed it. You require my approval before acting.

- Inform me of what you decide must be done. If I do not disagree with you, take action.

- Make the decision and take the appropriate action. Inform me of the results.

- Make the decision and take the appropriate action. Inform me of the results only if your decision was incorrect and the action was not successful.

Clearly, the amount of authority delegated to the subordinate increases as we progress downward through these various approaches. You will find each of these approaches to be effective at one time or another, depending on the importance of the decision and your confidence in the abilities of your subordinate. If a mistake could cause great damage to the organization and to your professional reputation and if you lack confidence in the ability of the subordinate, use the first approach: "Analyze the situation for me but I will make this decision." As your confidence in subordinates' abilities increases or as the riskiness of the situation decreases, use the other approaches. "Make the decision and take the appropriate action" would be suitable for assignments where a mistake would not be critical and where the subordinate, in your opinion, clearly has the ability to understand the issues and deal with them competently.

Also, recognize that you and your people need time to grow. It is unwise to define a complex set of duties and delegate them to an inexperienced subordinate. Not only is the probability of failure high, it is likely that the individual's confidence will be undermined for future assignments and that he or she will suffer personal insecurities. First assignments should be within demonstrated capacities and closely supervised. As the individual grows, more complex assignments may be delegated and more authority for decisions may be released.

Interestingly, most managers do *not* use all of these approaches. Their managerial style concentrates upon two or three. Harry Truman was extreme in his delegation. "You make the decision. We don't have to discuss it further. You are doing fine. I'll let you know when you are not." John Kennedy was the opposite. "Look into it. Get me the facts and write a proposal. I will decide." You choose what works best for you.

The Right Approach to Delegation

Here is a list of basic rules for proper delegation of authority. If you follow them, they will ease the difficulties of delegation for you and increase your probability of success.

Be absolutely sure of the degree of authority you are delegating and make certain the subordinate understands. If you are not giving authority for making decisions, say so. If you wish to be informed of the decision ahead of time, or merely the outcome after action has been taken, make sure the subordinate knows this.

Delegate in terms of expected results. Clarify the desired outcomes and how they will be measured or described. Do not delegate in terms of activities or you will drive your subordinates into the activity trap. Allow them the personal freedom to do the job the way they want to, within reason.

> *Delegation need not be difficult*

Give some "stretch" assignments. You are not merely trying to lighten your own burden. You are also trying to help your people grow. Routine dirty work won't accomplish this objective. Give some challenging assignments with a little excitement to them.

Tolerate mistakes and turn them into learning experiences. Occasionally your subordinates will fail. Analyze the reasons for failure. Learn from them. And be sure not to make the same mistake again. If the work is poor, hold the person responsible, but explain carefully why it was poor and what mistakes were made.

Match responsibility with authority. We have all been in those uncomfortable situations when we are held responsible for something we cannot control or influence. These are not desirable situations, and they are generally not beneficial learning experiences. Do not place your people in this sort of dilemma.

Retain some broad controls. Design some system for providing interim feedback so you are able to track performance or the lack of it. Progress reports, weekly discussions, etc., will allow you to monitor the assignment. Then use the exception principle and intervene only when necessary. Resist the urge for personal "on course adjustments" unless absolutely necessary. This is called "meddling by the boss."

Avoid "flip-flop" delegation. Once the authority has been given for a particular assignment, do not rescind the assignment and take back the authority. For example, a plant engineer asked a subordinate to examine the plant for safety hazards and recommend appropriate courses of action. Before the task was complete, the engineer learned indirectly that his boss, the plant manager, was extremely interested in improving the safety record of the plant. The engineer then saw this as a political plum and rescinded the assignment so he could do it himself. Bad management!

Trust your subordinates. Show that you have confidence in their abilities and judgment. Then make certain you explicitly recognize and reward competent performance.

Realize there are some tasks that should not *be delegated.* A conflict between two immediate subordinates should not be delegated to a third . . . or to one of the two involved in the conflict. Personal problems such as alcoholism should be retained by you. Other problems that are confidential in nature should not be assigned to someone else. And you should retain tasks that require unique technical expertise not possessed by your subordinates.

As you follow these rules and your experience accumulates, you'll probably find yourself becoming more comfortable with, and better at, delegation. In the long run, the better you are at delegating, the higher you will rise in your organization, as delegation becomes increasingly important at higher levels of management.

Summary

- Delegate to motivate your subordinates to grow and to free yourself to concentrate on more important objectives.
- Though you can delegate authority, you still retain responsibility.

- Plan to change any attitudes or lack of skills that are keeping you from delegating.
- Try different degrees of delegation depending on your comfort range, your subordinate's comfort range, and the situation at hand.
- Follow the basic rules for delegation, including emphasizing results, stretching subordinates, and maintaining broad controls.

Further Readings

1. A comprehensive discussion of proper approaches to delegation is found in R. Dreyfack, *How to Delegate Effectively* (Chicago: Dartnell Corporation, 1964).

2. For a thorough treatment of delegation, obstacles preventing its effectiveness, and examples of good and bad practices, see D. D. McConkey, *No Nonsense Delegation* (New York City: AMACOM, 1974).

41

5.

Controlling Performance

See everything. Overlook a great deal. Correct a little.

POPE JOHN XXIII

From this chapter you will learn:

- *What the steps in the control process are*
- *Why accurate and timely information is so important, and how you can get it*
- *How you take corrective action when performance does not meet objectives*

A famous economist once observed that the firm is run in the short term because "in the long run we'll all be dead!" A very important aspect of management in all organizations is *control,* assurance that proper progress is being made toward achievement of routine, recurring, ongoing, short-term objectives. Control must be exercised in the short term.

Lack of short-term controls was a major factor in the failure of the W. T. Grant Company, the large chain of five and dime stores. Bankruptcy testimony showed that buyers for Grant were often forced to ask suppliers about Grant's inventories because no internal information was available. Store managers were not allowed to purchase merchandise for their own stores and to control their own

Short-term controls are essential

stock levels. Suppliers were asked to bill more than the correct amounts and then pay the difference on the side to purchasing managers. Worst of all, many of Grant's debtors never paid their bills because the bills were never sent and no one discovered the discrepancies.

Obviously, that's no way to run a business! To be successful as a manager, you must maintain an effective level of control over the output your department is contributing to your organization's mission. The process of control is outlined in this chapter. The importance of being timely and accurate with your information is emphasized, and some suggestions are given to help you obtain the information you need. You'll also find a discussion here of how to get started if you find you need to take corrective action to get some aspects of your people's performance back in control.

The Control Process Has Four Steps

Recall that the black-box concept diagrammed and discussed in Chapter 2 included the two basic elements of output and feedback. Output and feedback are also basic to the four-step process of control. You carry out the control process as follows:

1. Define the desired levels of output.
2. Measure the actual performance.
3. Compare the desired and the actual.
4. Take corrective action, if necessary.

These steps are the same for control of any area of managerial concern. Whether you are controlling quality, inventory, cost, production, or finances, all are accomplished in this same fashion. It might even be argued that self-control and birth control consist of these same four steps. The control process can be visualized as shown in Figure 5.1.

The first step in the control process is the *specification of a desired result*. Call it a goal, a norm, a standard, a yardstick, a criterion, an objective, or a plan. The essential point is that *what ought to be* in terms of output is clearly specified. Without this specification there can be no control and without control the enterprise cannot survive.

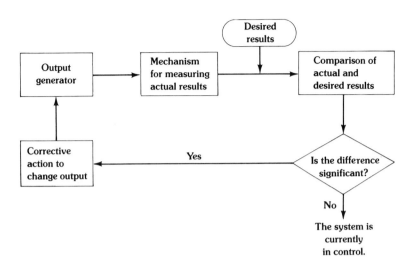

Figure 5.1 The control process.

From this viewpoint you can see why the critical nature of clearly defined and communicated objectives was stressed in Chapter 3, why the planned level of performance should be measurable or describable. If the desired performance is qualitative and vague, say "Improve morale of the department," how can the actual results be measured and compared and how can we possibly know if the difference is significant, thus indicating the need for corrective action?

The second step is *measurement of results, what actually is.* Of course, this measurement must be in the same dimensions as specified in the desired standard. A thermostat calibrated in Celsius will not be effective without conversion if the sensing thermometer is in Fahrenheit. Also, the measurement must be appropriately accurate. All measurement is subject to some error . . . accurate only to a limited degree. Thus, an important question for *every* manager becomes, "Is refinement of the measurement to improve accuracy or precision worth the cost to do so?" In some cases the answer is no. The critical issue is to get the measurement with some degree of accuracy to the proper manager who has the power to institute

Control cannot exist without a specific desired result

45

corrective action and do so promptly, before it is too late and the process is out of control.

The third step is *comparison of the desired and actual results.* If you know *what ought to be* and you know *what actually is* but you do not bother to compare in timely and intelligent fashion, you lose control. It is critical to understand that there is almost always a difference between desired and actual performance. The competent manager asks *beforehand* how large the variation can be before it becomes significant and must be dealt with. What are the limits within which the process may vary and still be considered "in control"? Every manager has more demands on his or her time than time available. If you allocate too much time and attention to trivial deviations from standard then more important areas will inevitably suffer. This is why defining objectives in terms of a range of values, as you've done in Chapter 3, is so important.

Compare and know what is significant variation

A significant difference between what you want and what you are getting is the definition of a "problem." If a control procedure is designed and managed correctly it will keep output within prescribed limits and avoid problems. It will predict early when output is headed for trouble so that actions can be taken early to prevent unacceptable levels. At worst, it will clearly indicate when a problem has occurred so that you may act accordingly. This is the culmination of the control process: *corrective action, taken when and if necessary.* When you identify a problem, you can then examine the variables, look for an assignable cause so as to remove or minimize its influence upon future output, restore the process to control, and solve the problem.

You should use this process of control in all key areas where you are responsible for outputs. You have already performed the first step by sitting down with your subordinates and agreeing upon specific objectives in key areas and in terms of a range of values. Your next step, measuring actual performance, is discussed in detail in the next section.

Timely and Accurate Information on Output Is Crucial

Measuring the output of your subordinates is easy if you have agreed-upon results and established a range of values. What is more challenging is receiving accurate information about their performance at timely intervals. For this you will probably have to rely on a management information system that may or may not have been designed with your needs in mind. If it was not, it may end up inundating you with data instead of telling you what you want to know in a usable form. To avoid this pitfall, you should sit down now and clarify your information needs. Ask yourself these questions:

- What are your key areas of responsibility for output?
- What information, specifically, do you need in these areas?
- What is the best form for this information (for instance, verbal descriptions, statistical graphs or charts, etc.)?
- How often do you need this information?
- Why do you need this information?

Make sure your information system meets your needs

A well-designed management information system should provide an early warning device for potentially fatal variances from agreed-upon performance and pinpoint responsibility for their resolution. For instance, one large computer manufacturing company has separated variances into *three* categories: (1) insignificant (routine status reports), (2) significant (worthy of analysis and change), and (3) "red bandits." The latter are truly critical problems that have the potential to be show-stoppers. The nature of this type of variance is so crucial that it is documented on red-bordered paper so as to alert people immediately. When a red bandit occurs someone is given immediate responsibility for its resolution. "You are responsible for this problem with our thermal system. Get on a plane today. Don't do anything else until the problem is solved. It *must* be operational in ten months!"

For routine objectives that are quantifiable, the agreed-upon range of values may be portrayed on a chart, with time added as a variable. The classic case in point is a control chart used in quality control. An example of a fraction-defective chart is shown in Figure 5-2.

Fraction defective is the indicator of output and is on the vertical axis. Upper and lower control limits and an expected level ($\bar{p}$) are established. Sequential sample values are tracked over time along the horizontal axis. On day 25 the process was out of control and days 17 to 24 showed a definite trend toward this problem. Corrective action was taken and the process returned to stability.

To keep track of output that is less easily quantifiable, you might find the chart shown in Figure 5-3 to be useful. It allows you

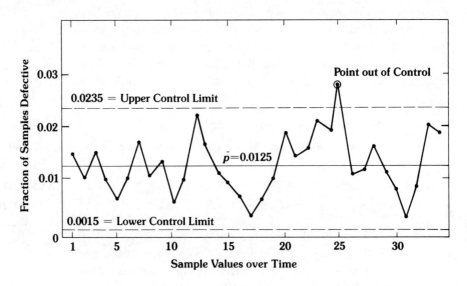

Figure 5-2 A fraction-defective chart.

to easily compare actual and desired performance so that you can quickly identify problems.

For example, a production control engineer might use this format as shown in Figure 5-4. The problem is then clearly defined. Over the recent past, back orders have been too high (40 percent), interim orders have been too high (4), picking time has been too long (9 per hour), and stock space is too small. The differences between the actual and desired values in the right hand column represent the problem, and these differences are significant in the mind of the engineer. When these differences are removed, the problem is solved. Obviously, this is a more useful definition than, say, "Parts inventory control must be improved."

These examples illustrate but a few of the many possible ways the information you require to compare actual performance with desired performance in order to identify problems can be organized. As important as the form in which information comes to you are the following criteria, which all management information should strive to meet:

Key Area of Responsibility	Actual Performance	Desired Performance
1.	1.	1.
2.	2.	2.
3.	3.	3.

Figure 5-3 A chart for comparing hard-to-measure performance.

- *Information should be reliable* — the same observations processed by other people or at other times should yield the same information.
- *timely* — the information should be available when a decision must be made.
- *economical* — the cost of the information should not be greater than its value.
- *necessary* — extraneous and irrelevant material should be absent.
- *sufficient* — the information should remove the maximum amount of uncertainty.
- *accurate* — the information should be free from error and in exact conformity with the facts.
- *usable* — the information should be free of distorting definitions and classifications, presented in understandable fashion, and should not require modification.

Management information must meet these criteria to be useful

Obviously, these criteria are somewhat inconsistent. For example, accuracy and timeliness may be maximized at the expense of economy. The most economical information in terms of information cost is no information at all. Thus, you should be prepared to make tradeoffs, recognizing that maximization of all seven traits is impossible.

Key Area of Responsibility	Actual Performance	Desired Performance
1. *Parts inventory control*	1. *40% back orders*	1. *20% back orders*
2.	2. *4 interim orders per month*	2. *2 interim orders per month*
3.	3. *Parts picking time: 9 per hour*	3. *Parts picking time: 12 per hour*
4.	4. *Stock space: 25,000 ft³*	4. *Stock space: 28,000 ft³*

Figure 5-4 An example of using the chart in 5-3.

If Corrective Action Must Be Taken

When you know the desired and actual outputs, compare them, and find the difference significant, you are faced with a problem and must take action to correct it. In this case, explicit definition of the problem is often critical. For example, a quality control problem was encountered in a process that produced printing plates. The rejection rate was excessively high. Tooling, raw materials, machine operators were all examined in an attempt to isolate a cause. It was then observed that metal chips removed in the process remained in the machine and damaged subsequent plates. The problem was now clearly isolated. The solution? Elementary. Recruit gravity as an ally by turning the plates and the machine upside down. The solution was fairly obvious once the proper problem definition had been made.

Once the problem has been defined, you need ideas, potential ways of removing or minimizing the difference between desired and actual output. You should take a creative approach to generating potential solutions; techniques you can use include brainstorming sessions and quality circles. These and others are discussed in depth in Chapter 8.

This step should be followed by a careful analysis of these potential solutions, a decision about which to apply, and application of the chosen one. Often several alternative actions are available and their impacts will be different. It is imperative for success in management that the correct action is selected more often than the incorrect one on the basis of insufficient information. Techniques you can use in decision-making are discussed in Chapter 9.

In general, then, the process you go through when you find a significant variance is the following:

1. Analyze the variance.

2. Isolate and identify problems.

3. Assess potential solutions.

4. Select a course of action.

5. Authorize and document action.

6. Implement the change.

A method for handling problems

Remember to single out for study not just negative variances, but positive ones as well. If the level of output is superior, look for assignable causes and see if you can perpetuate that set of conditions.

And watch out for the pitfall of attempting to solve problems by hiring more people. This solution will eat you alive in terms of budget and, in most cases, problems will not be resolved. The larger staff will merely make work for each other. The proper response when you are asked to assume a new responsibility or to solve a problem is "Give me a few days to prioritize what we are doing now. There may be some low priority tasks we can drop off the bottom in return for these new ones. I will come back and discuss these with you and, if it is humanly possible, we will assume these new responsibilities *without* adding new people."

Some Useful Generalizations About Control

As you follow the four steps of the control process, there are a few guidelines you should keep in mind.

Good control is not synonymous with maximum control. It is often possible to define strategic points where deviations are more

51

crucial and corrective action more effective. State governments do not place weighing and inspection stations at every possible entry. The costs of such a system would far outweigh its benefits. Instead, major highways are monitored and traffic controlled at these strategic points.

Suboptimization can and does occur in every organization. Suboptimization is choosing the best solution to a problem from the viewpoint of a subsystem but not from the viewpoint of the system as a whole. For instance, tight control of inventory levels may come at the expense of wide fluctuations in production levels. Production according to sales levels might minimize inventory but only at the expense of higher severance and training costs. Design specification of very fine tolerances may be desirable for customer service but may cause tremendous problems for quality control and production. Each subsystem of the organization optimized and controlled separately will likely result in a total performance at a lower level than if the system as a whole is optimized. Controls must be designed so as to minimize the undesirable effects of this suboptimization. This is a major function of management.

Controls must be flexible. An acquaintance of mine decided to obtain contract information from a large aerospace firm by phoning the purchasing agent rather than visiting him personally. When this aerospace firm received a large government contract and was buying heavily from my friend's company, my friend's long distance telephone expenses were several hundred dollars over budget. But his sales were several *thousand* dollars over forecasted levels. His boss complimented him on the sales performance but ordered him to reduce his telephone expense! Ridiculous but true. Even the best objectives need to be changed from time to time as conditions deviate from expectations. Admittedly, control systems cannot be continually changing but some replanning may be needed to reflect unforeseen circumstances. This is a judgment call on the part of the manager. Your control system, then, and your attitude should provide for some flexibility and resiliency while still retaining basic features.

Overcontrol can be hazardous to a manager's health. Overcontrol can occur in two ways: reaction rate (how strong the corrective action is) and reaction frequency (how often it is taken). Drastic changes in the system made frequently almost always result in overcontrol with undesirable consequences. The other extreme, of course, is taking no corrective action regardless of the situation.

The optimum balance is somewhere in between, the proper amount of correction made only when it is obviously justified.

Controls must be worth their cost. If significant deviations from the objective are inexpensive, an elaborate control system cannot be justified. A small firm cannot afford the elaborate control systems utilized by a large, complex firm nor does it need them. The competent manager always asks "What would be the consequence if I did *not* monitor this output? How much would it cost? What is the expense of controlling it? How do these compare?"

Contradictory controls should be avoided, when possible. It may not be possible for your subordinates to produce more volume at higher levels of quality and still stay within budget. A greater share of the market at higher prices may be unattainable. Thus, you should never specify performance criteria so that the only way your subordinates can look good in one area is at the expense of another . . . if it is possible for you to avoid this contradiction.

Controls should concentrate upon objective results. They should focus upon output and not people. Whether or not your subordinate is doing a good job should not be a matter of your own subjective opinion. It should be a matter of results generated relative to agreed-upon levels of output in key areas of responsibility.

Summary

- Managerial control consists of achieving what ought to be accomplished in terms of desired results.

- The basis of control is results-oriented objectives, accurate and timely measurement of actual performance, and appropriate corrective action when comparison shows that deviations are significant.

- Information about performance is crucial. Analyze your key areas and determine what information you need to achieve control.

- When performance varies significantly from objectives, you must decide among alternative solutions and take action to correct the situation.

- Good control isn't maximum control. Watch out for suboptimization. Stay flexible. Match costs and benefits of controls. Control output, not people.

Further Readings

1. An excellent collection of articles dealing with various aspects of the control process is R. J. Mockler, *Readings in Management Control* (New York: Appleton-Century-Crofts, 1970).

2. For a comprehensive treatment of managerial control with suggestions for improving your performance, see W. H. Newman, *Constructive Control* (Englewood Cliffs, N.J.: Prentice-Hall, 1975).

3. W. J. Reddin, *Effectiveness Areas* (Fredericton, Canada: W. J. Reddin, 1978) is an instruction manual describing the principles of measuring or describing output. Emphasis is upon results and suggestions are made for applying the principles to your particular job.

6.

Giving Feedback

Don't praise people too much, they may get cocky and sluff off. When someone really screws up, be sure to not only tell them, but everyone within earshot. This shows that you are both sharp and willing to face tough problems. Also, chew someone out for not having something done, and give them a week to do it. When you follow up and notice it has been done, don't mention it. Find something else. This way they'll always be on their toes.

JIM KUHN

From this chapter you will learn:

- *Why feedback is an important consideration for all managers*
- *How you can design a system to provide frequent feedback for your subordinates*
- *How you can reinforce good performance*
- *What the proper approaches are to periodic reviews and the annual review*

Though the comments cited above from Jim Kuhn's *Management by Hassling*[1] are intended to be ironic, many real-world managers inadvertently practice this philosophy. I was once supervised by a Dr. Dawson, Director of Research and Development, who had earned a doctorate in chemistry. After working for him for six months and feeling some frustrations over the lack of feedback, I entered his office one morning and hesitantly inquired, "How am I doing, boss?" He gave me an icy stare and said, "Don't ask! Don't ever ask! If you are not doing all right I will tell you. Otherwise, assume you are doing fine." In my opinion, this is not atypical of many managers with marginal administrative competence promoted into management because of superb technical skills.

A good manager gives feedback without being asked

Recall that one of the aspects of the workable, effective managerial plan presented in Chapter 1 was: *Provide frequent feedback.* Why is this important? If not done, what are the effects upon people in the organization? How can a manager do this best? Elaboration upon these questions and their answers is the subject of this chapter.

Why Is Feedback Important to You and Your Subordinates?

Experiments in sensory deprivation have shown that a certain amount of feedback is necessary for normal orientation and for mental health in the human being. One such experiment involved placing human subjects in a small isolated cubicle. They wore translucent glasses to reduce variability in vision. Their fingers were separated with cotton and their hands cuffed in cardboard. Total silence was maintained and temperature held constant. After a three-day period, tests showed significant reductions in intellectual and problem-solving abilities. Verbal, spatial, and mathematical skills were greatly impaired. Subjects showed considerably increased susceptibility to propaganda.

Eighty-six percent of the subjects hallucinated. The first symptom would be the appearance of dots and lines followed by objects against a dark background. Eventually, complex hallucinations occurred involving entire scenes. One subject could see nothing but eyeglasses no matter how hard he tried to get rid of them. Subjects had no control over the duration or content of these visions. Many could not sleep because of them, and several subjects left the experiment because they were so mentally disturbed by its effect on them. All required psychiatric therapy at the conclusion of three days of isolation and sensory deprivation.[2]

The human being is a complicated and demanding system. In order to exist in a healthy state, we require water, food, oxygen, sleep . . . and information. The subjects in the experiment could not maintain mental health for as short a time as three days without the input and feedback of their senses. The same generalization is accurate with regard to their professional performance.

Feedback is essential to the human organism

People have an innate, powerful, and continuing need to know how they are doing.

The annual performance review is not enough. In many cases, this amounts to finding out once a year about all the things they did not accomplish because they did not know what was expected. As the boss, you must not allow this to happen. It is unnecessary and drives morale and productivity to rock-bottom levels.

Particularly, you must pay attention to recent college graduates who are newly employed in your organization. For the previous several years they have been getting a constant stream of feedback. Every homework assignment, quiz, examination, written project, and final grade is feedback concerning the level of their performance. They may not agree with it, but, nonetheless, it is information on how the professors think they are doing or have done.

After years of this, the habit of frequent feedback is created. This is true whether your new employees exited at the bachelor's, master's, or doctoral level. If you ignore this need you will be depriving them of a basic requirement for emotional stability, and the consequences are predictable. If the feedback is nonexistent, they will be compelled to come to you and seek it, as I did with Dr. Dawson. "How am I doing?" is a sign you are not providing one of the essentials for your subordinates.

Building Continuous Feedback into the System

If feedback is so important and once a year is not enough, where do you start? You can start by realizing that every subordinate receives feedback every day: continuous, *environmental* feedback from customers, coworkers, suppliers, and the nature of the job itself. This type of feedback has a considerably greater effect on workers than periodic formal reviews because it is more frequent and it is more immediate. Considerable research has shown that

Environmental feedback has a greater effect than formal reviews

frequent feedback is much more effective in changing behavior and affecting performance than feedback that occurs only periodically, even if given in large quantities. And people are influenced more by feedback they receive immediately after doing something than by quarterly or annual reviews because it reinforces their behavior.

You have already turned these effects of continuous feedback to your advantage by agreeing upon specific objectives with your subordinates. Once you have agreed upon specific, measurable objectives for each of your personnel, in terms of a range, and have thus defined optimistic, realistic, and pessimistic levels of performance, the subordinate receives feedback *without* formal appraisal from you. Recall from Chapter 3 the hypothetical production worker who has as one objective "to produce X appliances per day." The realistic level is eighty, pessimistic is seventy-five, and optimistic is eighty-four. How often does this worker receive feedback on production volume? Every day! Does it come from you? No, it comes from a comparison of actual daily output vs. the agreed-upon levels, which you have promised will not be changed without a personal discussion with your subordinate.

By building this kind of continuous feedback into the system, you enable your subordinates to track their own performance and know precisely how they are doing and where they stand with you. They can grade themselves and know there will be no surprises when the formal appraisal comes around. It should come as no shock that performance and morale are considerably higher if this situation exists than if your subordinates enter your office with production figures once every three months and *then* find out whether or not they are in trouble.

Motivating with Rewards and Penalties

Behavior that results in a desirable consequence is apt to be repeated. That which results in an undesirable consequence tends not to be repeated. It is up to you to provide some favorable consequences when your subordinates achieve objectives and some unfavorable ones when they do not. If you do not have the authority or influence to provide favorable or unfavorable consequences of sufficient importance, you are not likely to obtain performance at the desired levels. *Reinforcement is terribly important.* Use the following principles to motivate your subordinates to improve their performance.

First, recognize that too few managers realize the tremendous power of positive feedback. *A good manager praises more than he or she criticizes.* An interesting experiment conducted in a large air-frame design group illustrates this principle. The engineers in this group were arranged randomly into three groups of equal size. For a period of almost one year, one group was given positive (favorable) feedback, one given negative (unfavorable) feedback, and the third group was ignored. Improvement in performance and productivity was monitored for all three groups. The results are shown in Figure 6-1. The group given praise and recognition increased performance two and one half times more than the group that was criticized and ten times more than the group given no feedback. Interestingly, no feedback (recall the sensory deprivation experiment) is significantly *worse* than criticism. At least someone cares enough to criticize rather than pay no attention at all!

Positive feedback gets results more effectively than negative or no feedback

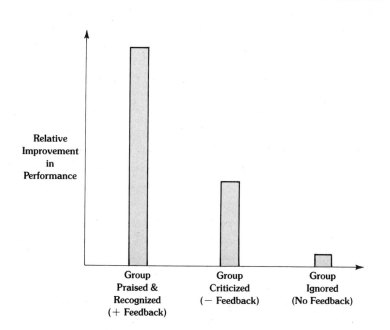

Relative Improvement in Performance

Group Praised & Recognized (+ Feedback)   Group Criticized (− Feedback)   Group Ignored (No Feedback)

Figure 6-1. Effects of different types of feedback on performance of groups of engineers.

Here is another example of the power of positive feedback. In a large oil refinery, I worked with a "turnaround foreman," Dan Day. His job was to supervise the annual shutdown of the refinery, the ensuing preventive maintenance, and the subsequent startup. His functions were very complex, indeed hazardous to some extent, and proper management of them was critical for operations of the refinery. Dan was super-competent. He made no mistakes. His human skills were excellent. His turnarounds were consistently flawless. I was not his boss, but I respected him and so one day I wrote a letter to Dan's superior:

> Dear Alex:
>
> From time to time, one has the pleasure of associating with an individual who performs his technical and managerial functions exceedingly well. I am writing to you to tell you that, in my opinion, Dan Day is one of these. Specifically . . .

The next morning Dan was in my office. He had tears in his eyes and his voice cracked as he said, "In fourteen years with this company, no one has ever done that for me. I came to thank you personally." This experience was very moving for me emotionally, and I felt very good about it. But there was another payoff. When my unit was involved with maintenance or turnaround, how much trouble do you think I had? *None!* Dan gave me preferential treatment over everyone else and would bust his rear end to see that I got what I needed, early. I wrote the letter because he deserved it, but both of us won in the end . . . and it took me about ten minutes to write the letter.

Positive feedback encourages cooperation

Try a little experiment in positive feedback. Surely there is someone working for you or with you who is doing an outstanding job. Today, why don't you tell them? Or write a letter to their boss as I did. It takes so little time and energy and the benefits are truly surprising.

> *Choose those who are performing well, walk up to them, and face-to-face tell them so!*

If you are blessed with a competent secretary or administrative assistant, you might start there. This person is an important determinant in your success as a manager but rarely receives positive feedback. Do it today. Watch for the surprise and, then, for the benefits. Try to make a habit of this. Remember, if you assume the right to criticize, you also assume the responsibility of praising when something is done right.

A second principle of motivation is that lack of performance not penalized will probably continue. If, in your best judgment, objectives are not achieved that should be, and there are no extraneous reasons except lack of performance on the part of your subordinate, you *must* let him or her know. But do so in private, not in public. Chewing people out in front of their peers is incredibly debilitating. They will not forget and it is not likely that their performance will improve because of it.

You must penalize lack of performance —privately

Third, choose appropriate rewards or penalties carefully. Subordinates have different needs and necessarily respond differently to reinforcement. Some possible rewards and penalties are listed below:

Rewards	*Penalties*
job security	probation, suspension, termination
money	less real income, or fining
recognition	criticism
praise and encouragement	disapproval
challenging assignments	undesirable assignments
promotion	demotion
improved working conditions	worse working conditions
status symbols	remove status symbols
sharing of confidential information	withhold information
favorable performance appraisal	unfavorable appraisal
greater scope of authority	removal of authority

There is an art to determining what rewards and punishments will be most meaningful to a particular subordinate. Avoid using the same reward every time. If you give the same praise to the same subordinate *every* time he or she generates a worthwhile result, the impact will eventually decline. The reinforcement becomes phony, inevitable, and worthless. An important corollary to this principle is that dealing out the same rewards to everyone, regardless of the level of performance, will destroy your subordinates' motivation for achievement. When worthwhile behavior occurs, try to reward it immediately with some positive reinforcement, but do it selectively.

Don't reward incompetence or penalize competence

Finally, avoid inadvertently rewarding a lack of performance and penalizing good performance. I know a weak manager who could not bring it upon himself to chastize or fire a subordinate who was not performing and had not done so for at least five years. The subordinate had been with this particular engineering firm for twenty years and was always at his desk. He came to work on time and never left early. He caused no human problems. But he never generated any worthwhile *results.* "How can I fire someone like Harry who has been a devoted, loyal employee for almost twenty years?" Instead, when the company received a contract for a portion of the Alaskan pipeline, Harry was promoted to Project Director and left for Anchorage. That is how his boss solved the problem. Nonperformance was rewarded. Harry is now a problem for someone else.

The other side of the coin was a financial officer in the same firm. A promotion was available and she applied for it. Her boss, who was new in that location, informed her that he had to remove her name from candidacy because he didn't understand the budgeting and reporting system and needed her help. She was too important and he could not function without her. Thus, competent performance was penalized. Do not reward nonperformance or punish performance in your organization.

Progress Reviews Are Worthwhile

You can use these principles of reinforcement to motivate your subordinates on an ongoing, day-to-day basis, and you can also apply them when it comes time for a formal performance appraisal. Most organizations require formal appraisals in the form of the annual performance review. However, it is generally your prerogative as the superior to encourage more frequent discussions of *progress* being made toward objectives on the part of your subordinates, and you should use this prerogative. You will find that quarterly reviews, as a minimum, are worthwhile.

At least *every* three months you ought to sit down face-to-face with your subordinates and compare actual performance with agreed-upon goals. "Here is where we agreed you would be in terms of this particular output. How are you doing? What can I do as your boss to help you achieve this objective? Is there something I can start doing that I am not now doing to help you? Is there something I should stop doing because it is hindering your performance? What should I do differently? What resources do you need?"

Review progress at least quarterly

Note that these questions allow the subordinate to open up and be honest with you, and thus require you to be secure and self-confident. If you ask what you should stop doing, your subordinate just might tell you! But that's good because the best way for you to look good is for your people to make you look good. If your behavior is hindering performance that will eventually reflect on you, isn't it better to find that out *now?* Also note that the above questions cast you in the role of *helper,* not tyrant. As stressed early in the book, your primary job, in addition to setting objectives with your people, is to assist them with advice, resources, guidance, and appropriate behavior so that the proper levels of output are achieved on time. Scheduling frequent progress reviews is an important part of doing that.

The boss as a helper

How often should these intermittent progress reviews be held? Their frequency is a function of two variables: *responsibility* and *confidence.* Many management authors define responsibility in terms like "the obligation to use power in the proper fashion as seen by those who bestow it." There is something very wrong with this definition. In addition to sounding like it comes from the priesthood, it is not operationally meaningful. How can you *use* this definition in the real world and, particularly, how can you use it to decide how often to meet with your people? You can't. Instead, try this one:

> *Responsibility is the amount of damage a person can inflict upon the organization if he or she makes a mistake.*

For each subordinate working for you, ask yourself this question: "If he or she really goofs, how much will it hurt?" If the answer is "A lot!" meet more often with him or her and use tighter controls to

63

Review frequency should be based on responsibility and confidence

minimize the probability of the mistake. If the answer is "Not too much," then meet less often . . . but at least quarterly. The greater the responsibility of your subordinate, the more frequent the formal discussions should be.

The second variable in determining the frequency of progress reviews is confidence. This refers to your faith and trust in the abilities of your subordinate. Admittedly, it is subjective, but also is probably based on his or her training and past track record. At one extreme, then, you might have a subordinate in whom you have great confidence but who does not have much responsibility. Meet with him or her quarterly. At the other extreme you might have one in whom you lack confidence and who can do great damage with a mistake! This is a dangerous situation for you since lack of performance on his or her part will reflect poorly on you and the organization. Meet often with him or her and track his or her output carefully. All other combinations of confidence and responsibility, of course, are between these extremes.

These periodic reviews should be oriented more toward *progress* than appraisal. Focus attention on results vs. commitments rather than on a personal, subjective evaluation of the worker. Where are the variations? Which are important and which can be ignored for the time being? What are the potential reasons for these variations? Examine key areas and indicators one at a time. Look for trends. What can be done now so significant progress can be made during the next period? Are there objectives that should be eliminated? Replaced by others? Realize that if a key area or indicator is changed it will likely have an impact on others.

Remember that the original agreement is *not* a legal contract with absolutely no room to maneuver. It is a commitment to achieve certain levels of output by a point in time. If unforeseen circumstances have occurred in the interim, allow a modification of the commitment unless it is critical. This will help convince your subordinates that you are a flexible, reasonable person.

Occasionally, a subordinate will fail. Then you must make a judgment call. Why did it happen? Was the objective unrealistically high? How important was it? How much of the failure was my fault? Do I punish him or her or forget it after it has been thoroughly discussed? What can be learned from this mistake? How can we prevent it from occurring again?

The Right Approach to the Annual Performance Review

The *annual* performance review involves aspects of progress but is more oriented toward *evaluation* than the more frequent progress reviews. If you have designed your system correctly and have held the intermittent progress reviews, the annual session should hold no surprises. Your subordinates know just about where they stand.

Set a specific time and date for the annual review and give your subordinates plenty of lead time to prepare. Do not stop them in the hall and say, "Come into my office for your annual performance review." You should ask them to prepare some notes about their commitments made a year ago, with a copy prepared for you. What overall progress has been made and where do problems exist? You should do the same in terms of reviewing the entire statement before the session begins. In planning for the review, you should ask yourself, "What do I really want to accomplish in the session?" Allow no interruptions (phone calls or visitors) during the interview. Treat it as an important part of your supervisory functions. It is!

Put your subordinate at ease. Do not force him or her into a defensive position at the outset. Rather, support him and allow him to go over the entire set of objectives and his notes before you ever discuss any specific one in detail. Encourage him to take the initiative and listen carefully to his comments. Seek clarification where needed and feed back your understanding of specific comments as he is making them so as to demonstrate that you really are listening and are interested.

Concentrate on results vs. commitments. Do not bring personality characteristics into the discussion. They are irrelevant. A research director in a very large pharmaceutical company in New Jersey told me of her annual performance review. At the conclusion, her boss admitted that every single objective had been achieved, several well above the optimistic level. But her superior gave her an upper-mediocre rating and only a cost of living increase in salary because "You could have done even better if your human relations skills were improved!" Don't ever do this. The appraisal is results-oriented, not trait-oriented, and it is not legitimate to intro-

Gear the annual review toward evaluation

Results count; traits don't

duce other variables that are a surprise to the subordinate and do not deal directly with results.

Systematically but sensitively explore deviations from objectives. Define significant problems and, one at a time, analyze potential causes, explore alternative solutions, and come up with an action plan for the next period.

Do not compare the subordinate to other people in the organization. They have different motivations and objectives. Sit down with your spouse in an annual performance review and compare him or her with other men or women, and see what happens. You would never do this, of course, so why do it with subordinates? It is not a rewarding or developmental experience. If your organization forces a system upon you that requires you to rank all the personnel in your area relative to each other, then minimize your use of this system. It may stimulate competition, but it will also minimize cooperation and personal growth and will maximize conflict. "Why should I help Tim even though I know more about that topic than he does? That will make him look better and may drop my ranking relative to him."

Do not return to prior periods and their reviews. There should be a statute of limitations of one year. "You screwed up in 1963 and now you have done it again!" is not fair. The performance appraisal is for the previous period only. Limit your discussion to this period unless there are very good reasons to return to prior periods in terms of their value in improving performance in the future. These are "sunk costs" and the subordinate has already paid for them.

A discussion of growth and self-development should be included in the appraisal. Where and how can the subordinate improve during the next year? Be specific though constructive. Ask for his or her suggestions. What objectives can we set for personal and professional growth, and how might we best achieve them? The next chapter covers this topic in greater detail.

Be certain to end the performance review on a positive, constructive note. Concentrate upon what was done right. Where are the pleasant aspects of the performance? Leave the subordinate with a good feeling about the whole experience, if possible, and with a desire to set and achieve more objectives and to grow while doing it. Build on strengths and don't belabor weaknesses. Remember, your major objectives are to evaluate fairly and improve future performance, not to castigate an offender.

Leave other people and other years out of this

Emphasize strengths and plan for growth

66

The organizational environment that will encourage achievement of worthwhile objectives is within your control to a great extent. The most prominent researcher in the area of achievement motivation, David C. McClelland, suggests three major characteristics of the achievement-oriented organization:[3]

Subordinates are allowed to set their own goals or plan a major role in the determination of these goals.

Goals are difficult to attain but are achievable.

Subordinates receive frequent and definite feedback about their performance while they are doing their job.

If you remember these characteristics while you manage, you will increase the probability of successful achievement of your own objectives.

Summary

- Feedback is essential to the human system to foster growth, performance, control, and emotional well-being.
- Feedback comes from both the environment and formal reviews. The former is more influential because of its frequency and immediacy.
- If objectives are known and are defined in a range, the system will provide the subordinate with feedback. It does not have to come from the boss.
- A good manager concentrates when possible upon positive feedback, gives negative feedback when it is warranted, chooses rewards and penalties carefully, and avoids penalizing performance and rewarding nonperformance.
- Hold intermittent progress reviews based on responsibility and confidence, realizing that the boss is the helper.
- Orient the annual performance review toward evaluation, schedule it ahead of time, do your homework, allow no interruptions, listen, put your subordinate at ease, concentrate upon results, learn from mistakes, avoid interpersonal comparisons, and discuss future growth objectives.

Notes

1. From J. Kuhn, *Management by Hassling* (New York City: Berkley Publishing, 1978).

2. Cited in B. Berelson and G. A. Steiner, *Human Behavior: An Inventory of Scientific Findings* (New York: Harcourt, Brace & World, 1964), pp. 88–92.

3. See D. C. McClelland, "Achievement Motivation Can Be Developed," *Harvard Business Review*, Vol. 43, No. 6 (Nov.–Dec. 1965), p. 6.

Further Readings

1. For a more comprehensive discussion of the annual performance review, see L. L. Cummings and D. P. Schwab, *Performance in Organizations: Determinants and Appraisal* (Glenview, Ill.: Scott, Foresman & Company, 1973) or G. S. Odiorne, *MBO II: A System of Managerial Leadership for the 80's* (Belmont, Calif.: Fearon-Pitman Publishers, 1979), Chapter 19, "The Problem of the Annual Performance Review."

2. For a pragmatic approach to the assessment of performance in R & D, see E. C. Galloway, "Evaluating R & D Performance — Keep It Simple," *Research Management* (March 1971).

3. An article discussing feedback and its impact upon performance is D. M. Herold and M. A. Greller, "Feedback: The Definition of a Construct," *Academy of Management Journal*, Vol. 20, No. 1 (March 1977), p. 142.

4. A novel and interesting treatment of performance problems in general is R. F. Mager and P. Pipe, *Analyzing Performance Problems* (Belmont, Calif.: Fearon Publishers, 1970).

7.

Developing Your Subordinates

Wherever we are, it is but a stage on the way to somewhere else, and whatever we do, however we do it, it is only a preparation to do something else that shall be different.

ROBERT LOUIS STEVENSON

From this chapter you will learn:

- *What you and your organization stand to gain by helping your subordinates grow personally and professionally*
- *How you can help your subordinates set objectives for growth*
- *How new graduates and mid-career subordinates differ from others you may be supervising, and how you can accommodate their special needs*

Our Western society is confronted with a furious storm of change. This storm is not diminishing but is, in fact, increasing in intensity. Knowledge increases exponentially, perhaps more so in many technical disciplines. It becomes more difficult to deal with one's environment and remain competent in one's discipline. A well-known living economist, Kenneth Boulding, observed that he was born in the *middle* of history. "Almost as much has happened since I was born as happened before!" He went on to observe that the world in which he now lives differs more from the world in which he was born than that world did from Julius Caesar's. Coping with this incredible rate of change requires adaptation, flexibility, and growth on the part of every individual if he or she is to be successful.

Growth and development has never been more important

There is a good deal of evidence that the 80s will be more oriented toward human development in the presence of rapid change than any other period in history. The human resources movement took hold in the 70s. Many major corporations, including AT&T, General Motors, IBM, Sears Roebuck, Xerox, Eastman Kodak, and 3M now have human resources staffs. The human resources department is much more than a personnel department, which historically has tended to be procedures and rule-oriented. The emphasis is now on developing policy with a commitment to forward-looking education, professional growth, and career development.

The increasing pace of change is just one reason for the growing importance of encouraging personal and professional growth in the work setting. There are a number of good reasons for you to consider this an important responsibility of your managerial position. In this chapter we will look at these reasons and give some practical suggestions about how you can encourage your subordinates' growth and development.

Why Developing Your Subordinates Is Essential

Developing your subordinates can have a number of important results for both you and the firm. When you consciously challenge and encourage your people to grow, you enable them to

- Keep up with change.
- Progress upward in the organization.
- Avoid tunnel vision.
- Maintain high job satisfaction.
- Increase their productivity.
- Replace you so you can move upward.

These outcomes are essential to the success of your department and your firm. They will be discussed one by one here.

Keeping up with change and progressing upward. The skills you and your subordinates now possess are not the skills you will need in five years. This is true first of all because of the storm of change spoken of above. The second reason your skills must change is that you will likely be in a different assignment that places different demands upon you. This is true whether you choose a managerial or a technical career path. If managerial, you must develop your skills in achieving results through others as you progress upward in your organization. If technical, you must maintain or improve your scientific competence by running at least twice as fast.

Avoiding tunnel vision. Technical types who devote their time to one particular problem area or specialty tend to develop skills and knowledge that make them experts in that area. Without conscious effort to expose themselves to other concerns, they rapidly develop tunnel vision, which prevents them from seeing beyond the special problems of their own departments. The more knowledgeable they are about their own specialty, the more narrow and one-sided they become and the more important their own department becomes. They become inflexible, less sensitive to the viewpoints of others, and less productive for the organization as a whole. The only way to avoid this trap is to continue to grow and broaden professionally.

Your skills must grow to move you upward and broaden your vision

Maintaining job satisfaction. In a recent survey of M.B.A.s, engineers, M.D.s, and lawyers the question was asked, "Are you getting what you want from your career?" Doctors and lawyers were most happy: seventy and sixty-three percent respectively replied yes. Of the four professions, the highest percentage of "no" responses came from engineers; almost half were unhappy with their careers. In addition, when asked if they expected to get what they wanted from their careers in the future, their negative response was highest of the four professions. Also, forty percent of the engineers said they would *not* continue in the same line of work if they were to come into enough money to assure financial security. When asked what single most important thing they wanted from their careers, what do you think the engineers replied? Lawyers and M.D.s both chose independence. Ranked above money, power, security, and independence, the engineers wanted intellectual challenge! The implications for you as a technical manager are obvious. Engineers exhibit more career dissatisfaction than other major professions and they *want* to be challenged. In a decade where dissatisfaction is high, personal and professional development

Intellectual challenge is essential

71

must be stressed and a major effort in this area must come from the corporation and from *you*.

Increasing productivity. There are also monetary and economic reasons in favor of professional development. Productivity in the United States has not kept pace with inflation; indeed, some argue that productivity in this country has begun to decline. Is this because of an increased orientation toward people vs. output? Is it because of OSHA, EEO, EPA, and other conflicting goals that take energy and effort away from production? These are difficult questions. But regardless of your feelings on these issues, the fact is that one way of increasing productivity and economic well-being is through professional growth with an emphasis on improvements in output per man-hour.

Replacing yourself. One last argument in favor of developing your subordinates is purely selfish. Many organizations will not promote anyone who has not trained a replacement! There is a syndrome in many bureaucratic organizations that is based upon a maximum desire for job security. "I will make myself indispensable. If no one else can do my job, then I cannot be fired. They *must* keep me because no one else can do what I do." Unfortunately, the manager who embraces this philosophy does not realize it is a two-edged sword. Being indispensable may, in fact, assure job security, but it also assures zero promotions. As a result of this manager's indispensable nature, he or she stays in the same job year after year with no threats . . . and no advancement.

In the final analysis, helping subordinates grow is a very important, inherent function of management. A good manager *must* be an educator of people. The most powerful career-building, learning experiences occur on the job. Everyday professional challenges are critical skill builders and important socializing influences. The job itself is more important than formal programs, classroom training, and professional seminars.

It is up to you to provide developmental experiences for your people and secure them for yourself.

Setting Objectives for Growth

Each of your subordinates should be committed to specific personal development objectives in addition to the ongoing objectives inherent in *every* job (which are the most important developmental influences). These personal development objectives should focus on growth that cannot be sustained exclusively through job-centered activities. Some of the objectives you might suggest to your subordinates are:

- Taking extension courses at a local university.
- Publishing a paper in a professional journal.
- Undertaking a personal physical fitness program.
- Completing a company-sponsored program.
- Studying some specific books on technical skills.
- Actively participating in a professional society.
- Designing and conducting training courses for others in the company.
- Participating in an executive development program.
- Speaking at a professional meeting or a university class.

The list could go on and on.

In order for your efforts to promote growth to be effective, you should keep the following guidelines in mind.

Development efforts must be directed toward some specific change in knowledge or skills. What change in terms of abilities, job performance, attitudes, or operational results is being sought? A useful question to ask is, "Which of the following are we trying to influence . . . improve performance on the present job, prepare the subordinate for future requirements of the present job, or prepare the subordinate for promotion to another job?"

Growth requires the explicit support of management. You, as the immediate superior, and other members of management must create a climate in which personal growth is not only desirable but necessary. Policies and procedures must not discourage creative efforts specifically aimed at personal growth. The most important individual in this regard is you, the immediate superior who establishes the managerial climate in which the subordinate must exist.

Your support and high expectations are necessary

The Pygmalion Effect can work for you. In Greek mythology, Pygmalion, King of Cyprus, made a marble statue of a woman that was so beautiful he fell in love with it. He wished and prayed fervently that the statue would come to life. She did, and Pygmalion married her. A powerful motivator is encouraging the subordinate to do well and, in fact, *expecting* it. If your expectations are within reason, the employee will live up to them. If you do not expect growth and superior performance, you will get neither. High expectations often become self-fulfilling prophecies by leading you to be more open with and supportive of your subordinates.

Motivation for growth is related to the probability of success. If growth objectives are set so high that they are impossible to achieve, the subordinate will lose all motivation. Similarly, if they are so easy that the probability of success approaches certainty, it is no big deal and motivation dies. The art is to stretch the subordinate but not break him or her.

Goals should be reasonable

Sufficient lead time should be allowed but a target time should always be set. Commitment requires setting a specific deadline. "I will accomplish these growth objectives by this target date." But the date should not be so immediate as to convince the subordinate that he or she cannot possibly accomplish that objective so soon.

Every effort should involve a follow-up. During periodic reviews and the annual performance review, you should discuss the growth objectives in detail. If possible, the relationship of the experience to job performance should be discussed. How did this growth objective help your subordinate achieve results, or how may it help in the future?

If appropriate for your organization, provide a choice between dual paths for individual growth. A traditional managerial ladder and an equivalent scientific/engineering ladder will offer parallel opportunities for subordinates who have significantly different career objectives. Without having these dual paths available, competent technical people may see management as the only way to progress upward, and this is often less than optimal for the organization and disaster for the individual.

The New Engineer/Scientist Has Special Needs

The frustrations of newly graduated engineers and scientists (ones who have been out of school, say, less than three years) deserve special attention in any discussion of professional development. There is ample evidence that the new generation of graduates differs from that of, say, twenty years ago. The new generation

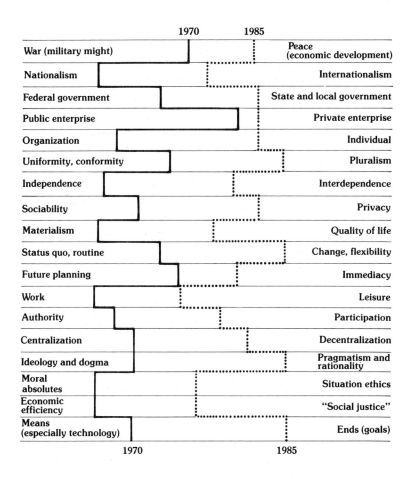

Figure 7-1. Profile of significant changes in value system, 1970 to 1985.

does not accept the notion that seniority is the best criterion for promotion. Demonstrated ability is more important. The new recruits are as competent and industrious as their predecessors but probably better educated. They are more independent and have a greater need for on-the-job challenge. They are more impatient with

75

incompetent management. Status quo is unacceptable. They are more protective of the natural environment, indeed, adamant about its preservation. They resist authoritarian management styles. Being informed is critical to them. Leisure time is very important because their life-styles are more diversified. They are more difficult to satisfy in a job assignment. When technical managers ignore these characteristics in new recruits, they are inviting serious problems.

General Electric studied eighteen values, paired them with their opposites, and researched their importance in 1970. Then, a "forerunner group of change leaders" were asked to estimate what their relative importance would be in 1985, and follow-up studies were performed at later dates. The results of this study (in highly summarized form) are shown in Figure 7-1.[1] Significant shifts are expected toward the values of individualism, participation, pluralism, decentralization, and ends vs. means (among others). All of these argue for a different style of management from what has been appropriate in the past.

So what are likely to be the major professional concerns of new graduates? A recent survey of 622 young engineers generated some surprising results. Their numerical replies are described verbally by me here:

New values demand new management styles

Professional Problem Area	Amount of Concern
no real problems	none agreed
technical preparation by the universities	no appreciable concern
psychological preparation by the universities	no appreciable concern
compensation	no appreciable concern
social adjustments outside work	no appreciable concern
on-the-job adjustments	BIG PROBLEMS! MUCH CONCERN!

Within the last category where the big problems lie, their concerns were concentrated in four areas:

• Learning how the company does things.

- Adjusting to a slower pace.
- Learning what is expected of me.
- Lack of opportunity to do sound engineering work.

Look at the new graduate's problem from his or her point of view. He or she has spent at least four years, maybe more, seeking a very challenging objective. Every assignment, quiz, examination, and class grade returned by the professor provides feedback about how he is doing. He is heavily recruited. Wanted, indeed, courted. In many cases, wined and dined. He chooses your organization from among many alternatives. Your recruiters have painted a very rosy picture because their success is measured in terms of hires. They do not have to deal with the recruit once he or she is hired. The engineer reports for work and is generally told something like, "Here is a technical manual. Read it. Come back in six months when you are smart!" This implies he or she can't handle it. He feels unused, unwanted, unchallenged, disappointed. Perhaps this is an exaggeration, but not much.

What can *you* do to ease the new recruit's frustrations? Here are some good rules to follow.

Don't overhire. If you do not have a challenging assignment for a new engineer, do not hire one. You will drive down profits, morale, and job satisfaction if you do. Don't play the numbers game just to increase the number of subordinates reporting to you.

Give a challenging first assignment. "Go read some stuff" is an insult. The first assignment is critical. Provide an opportunity for meaningful engineering work immediately, and, when questions do come up, provide reading material that will be of direct use. Be supportive when your new hire has questions or does not understand what is expected. If you wish, choose an initial assignment that is challenging but has low risk for you if not performed perfectly.

Challenge is the key

Don't underestimate abilities. Within some small bound of error, every graduating class is better than the previous one. Your new recruit can probably handle a lot more pressure, produce more good results, and solve more sticky problems than you think.

Give assignments in terms of results expected. Do not spell out what to do and how to do it. Explain what specific results you want and agree on a target date. Make certain the results are clearly understood. Get a commitment.

Learn new employees' expectations. Talk to your personnel department and recruiters. Examine their advertisements. See what they are doing. What was the new recruit promised? What are they selling? Ask recruits face-to-face what they expect in terms of initial assignments. Ask why they chose your organization.

Keep them busy. Most engineers and scientists admit they are working at some small percentage of their capacity. For the technical groups I have worked in, I would estimate the average to be between 20 and 40 percent. If their college training was good enough for you to hire them, they were kept busy, and are accustomed to it. This capacity for large amounts of work under pressure has been ingrained in them for years. You can destroy it in a matter of months. But do *not* keep them busy with menial tasks. "Busyness" for its own sake is bad news.

Recognize good work. Positive feedback when deserved is a powerful motivator.

Give feedback and support

Keep new hires informed about things that affect their performance. Let them know promptly about contractor developments, policy decisions, design changes, etc., so they will be able to adjust accordingly. And show them how their assignment fits into the entire project so they know their contribution is meaningful.

Demand quality. Don't let new employees get by with anything less than their best. But do not demand perfection every time. Admittedly, this is a fine line. When things go well, accept a little less than your rightful share of the credit. When things go badly, accept a little more than your share of the blame.

Develop a career worksheet. One page is sufficient. Include employee background and special interests. In five years, where does he or she want to be? Does he or she wish a technical or managerial career path? What specific things can be done during the next year to further this plan? What can you both do *this year* to assure professional growth? Write down the answers to these questions. Review them with your employee at least every quarter and go over the worksheet in detail at the end of the year, preferably during annual performance review. Follow through. Do not allow *any* of your technical subordinates to get by without this worksheet.

Recognize that if you follow the above suggestions, there is some risk for you. Recruits will make mistakes that will reflect adversely on you. Some may wish to grow through a transfer to another department, and you will lose them. Some will return to a university for formal training. These are some of the prices you must pay for helping people grow.

The Mid-Career Subordinate Also Has Special Needs

In addition to newly graduated subordinates, you may also inherit some mid-career partners. Realize that several potential managerial problems in technology-oriented companies are related to age differences. For example, personal development efforts of most organizations are often biased in favor of younger employees. "We've got to do something for those young people. They are the future of the company. Besides, George has been around here for a long time and is too valuable to spare for a week. We can't do without him. I'll send young Jim to San Francisco for that training instead of George." This problem (from George's point of view) is magnified by salary compression. The older employees see new graduates brought in at almost equivalent salaries.

What about the forty- or fifty-year-old engineer or scientist in your organization? This mid-career type tends to be more self-reflective and introspective than the new graduate. Money is usually less important to him or her than it was twenty years ago. There is now a strong questioning of occupation and life-style. He asks himself, "Is it too late to make a major change in my career?" Many experience a mid-life crisis because they cannot achieve a comfortable transition from youth to middle-age. Their lives are ones of quiet urgency. This syndrome is especially evident among engineers or scientists who feel they have plateaued, are underutilized, and are unchallenged. The big fuss made over newly hired engineers only makes matters worse.

Understand that this problem exists for your mid-career subordinates. You may even face this problem yourself. Do not ignore these people. The retention of these employees and their continued development is of paramount importance for your organization. It is often the most competent employees who reassess their careers and feel unchallenged because their competence exceeds their responsibilities. The incompetent ones have already left, voluntarily or otherwise, or do not experience any crisis because they feel sufficiently challenged. In many cases, it is a better investment of time and money to help competent mid-career people grow. They are more likely to remain with your organization, and if they are dissatisfied, the young employees will be smart enough to see it. Low morale and job dissatisfaction on the part of the older employees will have the predictable undesirable effect on the younger ones.

Mid-career employees need challenge and support too

79

Consider the concept of career revitalization. What goals can be set for mid-career growth? What career path alterations can be made? In order to revitalize, what can be done now? Next year? How can you help? Think in terms of a career shift, not merely next year. Realize that job assignment and challenge are the most important influences in personal development, even for mid-career types.

For example, consider a research chemist I worked with for several years. Norm was an exceptional polymer chemist but after fifteen years in that field, he felt burned out. It seemed to him that he was dealing with the same problems, the same formulations, the same colleagues, and the same physical environment. He was in a rut. Fortunately, he discussed this with his boss and admitted he was thinking of leaving for another company. Because Norm was a valuable employee and was congenial and an extrovert, his boss arranged an experiment with the sales manager. Norm would act for a six-month period as a technical support advisor for the special products department. He would accompany salespeople when customers had special requests with technical overtones. Norm was the buffer between sales and engineering. Norm's performance was exceptional, bringing in considerable new business. Moreover, his morale and job satisfaction improved significantly and six months later his trial position was made permanent.

Finally, understand that most managers and most organizations are singularly unsuccessful in solving this kind of problem. If you are successful in this regard, you have developed a significant competitive edge.

Summary

- Adaptation, flexibility, and growth are essential if one is to be successful in these times of rapid change. One of your key responsibilities is to encourage and support your subordinates' growth.

- Engineers and scientists want and need intellectual challenge. Make sure you provide them with it, and with other opportunities to reduce tunnel vision, move upward, and increase their productivity.

- Besides output objectives, you should agree upon personal growth objectives with each subordinate. Set specific and achievable objectives with a time limit, and review and support your subordinates' efforts toward them periodically.

- Put yourself in the shoes of your new recruits, and try to give assignments that are challenging and in line with their expectations.
- Be sensitive to the continued development needs of employees in mid-life transition, and set goals for career revitalization.

Note

1. Reprinted from *Michigan Business Review* by Ian H. Wilson (Ann Arbor, MI: The University of Michigan, DIVISION OF RESEARCH, GRADUATE SCHOOL OF BUSINESS ADMINISTRATION, July 1974), p. 24, Figure 4, by permission of the publisher. Copyright 1974 by the University of Michigan. All rights reserved.

Further Readings

1. Two excellent sources for additional information on career management and development are: M. A. Morgan, *Managing Career Development* (New York City: D. Van Nostrand, 1980); M. Jelinek, *Career Management for the Individual and the Organization* (Chicago: St. Clair Press, 1979).

2. For an interesting study dealing with the special problems of professionals in your field, see B. McKelvey and U. Sekaran, "Toward a Career-Based Theory of Job Involvement: A Study of Scientists and Engineers," *Administrative Science Quarterly*, Vol. 22 (June 1977), p. 281.

3. An informative and interesting treatment of burn-out and managerial obsolescence is K. E. Warren, T. P. Ferene, and J. A. Stoner, "The Case of the Plateaued Performer," *Harvard Business Review* (January–February 1975), p. 30–40.

8.

Encouraging Creativity and Innovation

. . . For most of us, creativity is more of a dull glow than a divine spark. And the more fanning it receives, the brighter it will burn.

JAMES L. ADAMS

From this chapter you will learn:

- *Why innovation is important, and how you can turn it into an objective*
- *Which arrangements and attitudes stimulate creativity, and which stifle it*
- *What specific techniques you can use to spark creativity in your department*
- *What causes resistance to innovation, and how you can overcome it*

Just as people must continue to grow and develop if they are to meet the new demands and challenges of the times in which we live, so must organizations make a commitment to innovation if they are to survive and prosper. There is no question that nurturing creativity and generating innovation is difficult, requiring imagination and effort. Changes in methodology are not only challenging but risky since people are required to make commitments in areas where outcomes are uncertain. But without these commitments to improvement, individuals and organizations become stagnant, oppressive, and vulnerable to competitors.

In modern organizations, innovative thinking is becoming more important all the time. It is needed both to solve problems and to take advantage of opportunities. New products, policies, services, and processes must be continuously generated if the organization is to improve and keep its competitive edge. Managing this necessary innovation as well as overcoming resistance to the resulting changes are the topics covered in this chapter.

How You Can Set Objectives for Innovation

You've learned so far in this book that agreeing upon routine objectives with your subordinates is necessary to assure that day-to-day, month-to-month operational results will be achieved. This is necessary, but in itself it's not enough.

> You must also make a commitment to introduce new ideas and improve the overall nature of your department, and you must achieve these results through your subordinates.

Therefore, you need to know how to help them set objectives for innovation as well as for routine outputs.

Objectives for innovation can be set either in response to problems that have been identified or to opportunities that present themselves. A well-stated innovative objective should name as a minimum:

New ideas are needed to solve problems and seize opportunities

- A specific result.
- A target date.
- Any cost associated with the innovation (dollars and/or time).

I had the appalling experience of witnessing the death of an electrician who tried to hook up a power analyzer to a 485-volt switchbox without pulling the master switch. Because it was the first fatality in this particular magnesium reduction plant, the plant manager was somewhat confused as to who should do what. A safety engineer saw in this a need for emergency reporting procedures and wrote the following properly stated innovative objective:

> Write an "Emergency Procedure Manual." It must contain the details of:
>
> **1.** Whom to notify (and in which order) in the event of:
>   a. Accidental death on our premises of either a company employee or other person.
>   b. Accidental death of an employee while away from our premises but on company business.
>   Included should be company officials, county/state/local officials, next of kin.
>
> **2.** Whose responsibility it is to handle the notification and how it should be handled.
>
> **3.** Emergency procedures to be followed and parties to be notified in the event of fire within our premises, destruction of company property, or civil disorders interrupting our normal business patterns.
>
> The manual should be prepared in final form in four months and be in use in six months time. The cost should not exceed five man-days.

The commitment is clear. The objective will be accomplished when the manual is completed in final form and contains the specifics cited above. The plant manager can now evaluate the commitment in terms of content and can add or delete procedures. Also, he or she can evaluate the costs and benefits. Is this innovation worth five man-days? Obviously, this manual was supplemented by a thorough investigation of the practices of company electricians in order to prevent subsequent injuries or fatalities.

You might consider using the above format with your subordinates. What new idea do you plan to work on, study, assess, suggest, or install in your areas of responsibility during the coming year? Think of this as a new idea outside your regular responsibilities that will add to results or improve the overall nature of your organization. Describe in detail your idea, your target deadline, the specific results you want to achieve, and the estimated cost.

Set some specific objectives for innovation

Set the Stage for Creativity

Creative organizations, those in which innovation goes on continually, have certain characteristics. As a manager, you can reproduce many of these in your own department. To the extent you are able to set the stage, your organization will stimulate innovative behavior. Among the most important characteristics are the following:

- *Authority in creative organizations is decentralized.* Creative individuals are suppressed by an authoritarian atmosphere. Their thought processes and intellects are less disciplined, and thus they do not perform well in a "tight ship" outfit.

- *Channels of communication are kept open and secrecy is minimized.* Mutual support, cooperation, and sharing of information are the norms. Free discussion of ideas is encouraged.

Some traits of a creative organization

- *Risk is recognized as a price that must be paid.* Taking intelligent chances is rewarded, not stifled. When mistakes are made, subordinates are not penalized. Rather, the issue becomes, "What can we learn from this mistake so it becomes a positive learning experience, not to be repeated if possible?"

- *Idea-generating devices are used extensively.* Brainstorming, quality circles, suggestion systems, checklists, and other similar approaches are commonplace.

- *Routine duties are defined, ranges set, and then delegated to others* in order to free the creative powers of the most highly trained and talented individuals (rather than tie them up with details and force them into the activity trap so they do not have time or energy left for innovation).

Besides cultivating these characteristics in your department, you can also set the stage for creativity by learning to recognize and overcome certain attitudes and habits that block creativity. Every individual comes up against barriers to creativity, though they vary from one individual to another and over time for a particular individual. Some of the most common barriers are the following:

- *An inability to define or recognize the real problem or opportunity that demands innovation.* This block is common. Scientists and engineers cannot innovate and solve complex problems if the *real* issues are not properly defined.

- *The tendency to artificially limit the search for alternatives.* The creative individual uses undisciplined exploration in decision making and problem solving. Ideas are unusual, even bizarre at times. Search becomes a most important part of innovative thinking. No holds are barred, and no unnecessary assumptions are made.

Some common barriers to creativity

- *A preference for order.* Engineers tend to think that organization is good and chaos is bad. Yet much worthwhile innovation emerges from a chaotic situation. One might even argue that innovative solutions are often intended to create some order out of messy situations. Furthermore, real-world problematic situations involve uncertainties, conflicting arguments, and unorganized information. One must learn to be comfortable with disorder. It is a fact of life in any complex organization.

- *A tendency to pass judgment too quickly.* Immediate judgment is often wrong and damaging to creativity. Psychologists who have studied creativity have long known the value of incubation. Many examples are documented wherein brilliant ideas came to researchers at night retiring for sleep or while loafing on the beach or early in the morning while shaving. Thus, one important characteristic of the creative individual is the suspension of judgment and the avoidance of early commitment to a course of action.

- *Comfort with the status quo.* We all have a tendency to become comfortable with the status quo. Disappearing into the woodwork, avoiding waves, and maintaining a low profile is common among technical managers and subordinates. Our culture has many phrases to justify this behavior pattern. "Let sleeping dogs lie." "Don't rock the boat." "Don't make waves." "Be seen but not heard." The competent manager will not encourage this approach; indeed, will not allow it. Conscious questioning is an asset to be cultivated. *Why* do we do things this way? *What* if we tried another way? *Why not?*

These barriers, once recognized, can be overcome. A number of devices have been developed by creativity experts to enable people to get around their blocks. Some of these are presented next.

Techniques You Can Use to
Stimulate Creativity

The vast literature that deals with creativity has proposed that the creative process consists of the following four steps:

The four steps of the creative process

1. Preparation — assembly of material, analysis of available information, observation of a need.
2. Incubation — letting up, relaxing, inviting illumination.
3. Insight — birth of ideas, possible solutions.
4. Verification — experimentation, testing the idea, development of the final option.

Many techniques have been suggested to facilitate this process. For example, questioning the status quo facilitates observing needs, so checklists have been developed that are useful in stimulating this questioning. This one, developed by Osborn, suggests different operations that can be performed on existing elements to improve them:[1]

- *modify* — add something
  — more time, greater frequency
  — make stronger, higher, longer, thicker
  — duplicate, multiply, exaggerate

Checklist of ways to change the status quo

- *minify* — subtract something
  — make smaller, condense
  — omit, streamline, split up, put under
  — lower, shorten, lighten

- *substitute* — another process, ingredient, material
  — another place, approach, form of approach

- *rearrange* — interchange components
  — other sequence, schedule, other pattern layout
  — other person

- *reverse* — transpose positive and negative
  — try opposite, turn backward, upside down
  — reverse role

- *combine* — combine uses, purposes, ideas, approaches

- *put to other uses* — new ways to use
  — other uses, if modified
  — what else is like this

New ideas can be checked against a list like this:

- Will my idea improve methods of operation, maintenance or construction? Will it increase production? Improve quality? Improve safety?

- Does it reduce waste or conserve materials? Eliminate unnecessary effort? Reduce cost?

- Will it improve office methods or reduce paperwork? Improve working conditions?

If the answer to any one of these questions is yes, the idea may be constructive and should be pursued.

Brainstorming is another technique that is helpful in stimulating new ideas if used correctly. A group of bright people, say ten plus or minus a few, is assembled and allowed to innovate. Several rules must be observed if this approach is to be effective:

- Your initial objective is *quantity of ideas.* Quality will follow. Nothing is ruled out. Criticism or rejection is not allowed.

- *Modification* of an idea is encouraged.

- *Wild, unusual ideas are sought.* Free, imaginative thinking and humor are desirable.

- *Judgment is deferred.* Ideas are not adopted until a later judicial session when poor ideas are rejected and good ones are acted upon.

Brainstorming encourages free thinking

Several variations of brainstorming have been very successful. In one, the group is shown a waste product that is currently discarded. The objective of the session is to generate ideas for the use of this item. Another approach has an objective of tearing down an existing product. What are its weaknesses? Name everything possible that is wrong with it. Afterward, ways of improving the product by removing the weaknesses are examined.

When used correctly, brainstorming has real potential for stimulating creativity. Admittedly, the technique does not always work. Some people view it as "weird" and "kinky." Others claim it is a waste of time. In many cases, both these criticisms are valid. However, the benefits of brainstorming are real and well documented in the literature of creative problem solving such as the Osborn work cited at the end of this chapter.

An interesting and productive variation of brainstorming has achieved prominence recently in the United States. Many major companies have found the concept of *quality circles* to be worthwhile in improving productivity and morale. The basic idea originated with the American management expert W. Edwards Deming, who was especially successful in introducing it in Japanese industry. Now it is also being embraced with enthusiasm by American firms. Westinghouse has over 1000 circles operating in 200 plants. Honeywell has 469 circles. Textron, Hercules Powder, General Electric, North American Phillips, and General Motors are examples of other firms committed to the idea.

The concept is simple, based upon a participative management philosophy. A group of five to ten volunteers from the plant floor, production line, or research laboratory are assembled regularly and given an hour or so to sit around and discuss how to make things better. But they do more than talk. They think scientifically and creatively as a group. They identify problems, rank these problems in terms of importance, generate potential solutions, and propose actions to be taken by workers and management.

Certain principles must be followed if your company's use of quality circles is to succeed:

- Members of QCs must be *volunteers.* Productive solutions will not result if workers are forced to participate as "one more requirement for keeping my job."

- *Five to ten members* per group is optimal. Fewer participants will not generate the diversity of inquiry that is necessary. More than ten is unwieldy and time-consuming.

- Structure the group with *diversity.* Include an engineer or a time-study expert or a computer systems expert or a secretary.

Quality circles can solve problems and boost morale

- Beforehand, appoint a *facilitator* who is a cheerleader, teacher, technician, and part-manager of the group. The facilitator must be someone who is able to tolerate unstructured thinking and communication but prevent the group from wandering off into unproductive tangents.

- After an initial presentation by the facilitator concerning the nature of the circle, the structured part begins. *Each person talks in turn,* states one idea, and then shuts up until his or her turn comes around again. The majority rules in identifying and prioritizing problems. The discussion is not allowed to stray from the subject at hand, the jobs of these persons.

- The major objective is to *pinpoint a specific, important problem* and solve it.

- *Costs and benefits are not considered.* The circle's mandate is creativity, not justification of its existence by generation of cost-saving ideas.

- Once a group has defined a problem, analyzed it, and developed a potential solution, *the package is presented to management.* It is critical for management at this time to play by the rules. The reply must be either, "Good, let's do it," or "No, we can't do it and here are the reasons why." Procrastination or unjustified rejection is not acceptable.

- Team members *participate on company time* and, if this is not possible, they are paid for overtime.

Skeptical? At one company, a supervisor who stated she had no problems at all was convinced nonetheless to start a quality circle. Her group identified twenty-two problems the supervisor never knew existed as well as several potential problems that would occur if the system remained the same. Hughes Aircraft has slashed defective production since their program began. General Electric conducted a survey of worker attitudes at three separate appliance factories before setting up quality circle programs. Half of the workers surveyed were to be involved in quality circles and half were doing similar tasks but were not included as circle members. Six months later the same workers were surveyed again and there was a 15 percent "positive change" in the attitudes of circle-group members and a 15 percent decline in control group attitudes.

Thus, in addition to dollar-saving ideas and improvements in design and quality control, quality circles seem to contribute to increased esteem, a sense of identity, higher job satisfaction, lower absenteeism, lower turnover, and fewer labor disputes. People are convinced that their opinions are important. Someone up there is listening. Quality circles encourage involvement, open lines of communication, and acknowledge that people are interested in doing something to improve their own work. Interestingly, one expert claims that four out of five problems dealt with by quality circle groups can be solved and the solutions implemented by the workers themselves without the involvement of management.

Training of the facilitator and team members is essential. Companies with successful programs send the facilitators to one- or two-week training sessions. Other team members receive at least five or six hours' training in problem-solving techniques. Many companies send facilitators to refresher courses after the QC programs have begun. Untold numbers of programs have collapsed because participants were not trained and, therefore, initial efforts were failures.

You may try all or some of the techniques described in this section with your subordinates. When your group starts coming up with innovative ideas and solutions to problems, be prepared for the next problem that will face you. This problem is the topic of the next section.

Innovation Is Often Resisted

Organizations and their members have an inherent resistance to change. The status quo is more comfortable. Human nature has much in common with a gyroscope, which has a built-in inertia opposing change in direction. This resistance is especially strong when the change is major and sudden.

In analyzing the underlying reasons for this inertia, it is useful to distinguish between resistance on the part of those managers who have the authority to institute change and those who are subject to it. Personnel who have the power to decide whether or not the proposed change is made may reject it for any of the following reasons (or some combination of them):

Some reasons why managers may resist change

- Regardless of difficulties with the current system, it probably *does* work. *"Why change to a new system that may not work when the current one is acceptable?"* This uncertainty is compounded by an aversion to personal risk. Any change that is more than minor exposes a manager to criticism if things go wrong. The tradeoff, then, is between an existing inferior approach that is certain and a potentially superior approach that is uncertain. Many managers cannot deal rationally with this issue.

- A manager who has developed years of experience and related skills in the current system may feel a *fear of being made obsolescent*. Thus, he or she may resist the change because it will force him to develop new skills that he feels he may not be able to acquire or that will require additional effort to acquire.

92

- An insecure manager may foresee a *loss of authority or job content*. If the change, for example, has an advantage of reducing the size of the work force, the manager may see this as a loss of status and responsibility. An implicit assumption on the part of some managers is that their importance is directly proportional to the number of their subordinates. Job dilution or reduction in workforce, therefore, is to be strongly resisted.

- When the change is proposed by an outside "expert," as is often the case, the manager may see the proposal as *a threat to his or her prestige* in the eyes of his group. If an engineer designs the new system and recommends a change, the superior may feel his or her people will interpret this as an inability on his part to see the need for the change and institute it himself. This is often magnified by a personality conflict between the expert and the line manager. This conflict is especially common if the superior designed the current system and thus views the proposed change as personal criticism.

- The manager subject to the change may not have participated in the design of the new system. Therefore, he or she may not understand it and his or her resistance may be a face-saving instinctive reaction. This is also the major reason why some systems that are changed radically result in failure or underachievement of objectives. *The person designing the system is not the one who must use it.* The experts design it and then move on to other projects.

- *The timing of the proposal may be inopportune.* Production, quality, labor union, or personal problems may be consuming the time and energy of the manager. What he or she does not need is an additional problem and exposure to risk.

- New, inexperienced workers may find the basic reason for resistance is *lack of confidence in their technical abilities* and personal judgment. "You are still wet behind the ears and do not realize all the reasons why this will never work!"

Those employees subject to the change but with no authority over the decision may resist for many of the above reasons. Exposure to risk, job dilution, loss of expertise, lack of participation, lack of confidence, and inopportune timing may all be factors. In addition, the following causes may contribute to resistance:

- There may be *peer pressure* in the work group. Members of groups do not want to offend fellow workers. Every group has a norm, a prescribed code of behavior. Changes that may violate these patterns will certainly cause adverse opinions and resistive reactions in the group affected by the proposed change.

Some reasons why subordinates may resist change

- *Economic insecurity* may be a factor. Will the change open the possibilities of reclassification or a reduction in status or take-home pay? This is particularly true if the change involves a new work method and, hence, a new standard for production. "Now I will have to work harder and produce more for the same (or even less) pay. No way, baby!"

- *Executives, outside experts, and especially engineers are always suspect.* In fact, they are usually quite unpopular among non-technical fellow workers. This suspicion and lack of popularity are magnified if a tactless approach is used to communicate the change.

How to Overcome Resistance to Innovation

Plan the introduction of your innovation carefully

You should seriously consider the following suggestions in planning the introduction of any innovation that involves a change in methods or policies.

Keep it simple. People may not understand your proposal if it is too complex. Very often if you reduce the complexity by 80 percent, you lose only 20 percent of the advantage. It is better to have a slightly suboptimal system that is implemented than a perfect system that is rejected or misused.

Actively sell the innovation. All the principles of salesmanship apply. Pinpoint the profits. What are the advantages to the organization, to you, and to the workers? Explain the need for the change. Communicate carefully the nature of the change. Tailor your presentation and written documentation to the nature of your audience. Give condensed versions to top management. Give more detail to those who must operate the system and make certain they understand the nature of the proposal and the personal advantages to be gained by them if the system is adopted and used effectively.

Do not underestimate the hourly worker. They very often have the power of determining whether or not your innovation is a success or an abysmal failure.

Involve others by allowing them to participate in the project. People work harder to make an innovation successful if they have been involved in its design. Consult workers, inspectors, supervisors, and other managers. Ask for their counsel and advice. What information do they have? What opinions? Suggestions? Include their worthwhile contributions. Be tactful and open to suggestions. Do not make up your mind ahead of time and then sell a preconceived system no matter what anyone says.

Institute the system in stages. This is especially good advice if changes are major. A common pitfall is to say, "We are on the old system Friday. On Monday the new system will be in effect!" Concentrate upon first instituting aspects of the proposal that will have the greatest immediate advantage. Where will the payoffs be visible as soon as possible so as to positively influence the largest number of people at the least personal risk? For example, a new inventory control system might be instituted as the items come up for reordering, one at a time, rather than placing, say, 22,000 inventory items immediately under the new rules for order point and order quantity. Perhaps only the high volume or high dollar value items should be included in the new system, leaving other unimportant items on the old system.

Provide thorough training in the new procedure, making certain that the innovation is understood and the requisite skills are being acquired by those who must use it.

Have the changes instituted by the immediate superiors of those who are affected by the changes.

You must also realize that, over the long term, change and innovation are a way of life. It is inevitable for growth and avoidance of stagnation. Thus, you must condition yourself psychologically to live with change and all of its implications.

Summary

- Innovation and creativity keep a firm competitive and enable it to solve problems and seize opportunities.
- A well-stated innovative objective is composed of a specific result, a target date, and an estimated cost.
- A creative organization is normally less authoritarian and more open, tolerates risk, uses idea-generating systems, and frees people from mundane routine duties.

- The creative individual avoids immediate judgment, thus inviting illumination; recognizes the *real* problem; uses undisciplined exploration; tolerates disorder; and questions the status quo.
- Checklists, brainstorming, and quality circles can be used to stimulate creativity in an organization.
- Organizations have a built-in resistance to change. Causes of this inertia may be different for people who institute the change and for those subject to it.
- Techniques for overcoming resistance to change include keeping the change simple, selling the innovation, involving others, and instituting the change in stages.

Note

1. From A. F. Osborn, *Applied Imagination* (New York: Scribner's, 1960).

Further Readings

1. An interesting and thought-provoking work on innovative thinking is J. L. Adams, *Conceptual Blockbusting* (San Francisco: San Francisco Book Company, 1976).
2. A practical guide to increase your expertise in dealing with change is E. Burack and F. Torda, *The Manager's Guide to Change* (Belmont, Calif.: Lifetime Learning Publications, 1979).
3. A. Levenstein, *Use Your Head: The New Science of Personal Problem-Solving* (New York: The Macmillan Company, 1965).
4. Another excellent work especially useful for scientists and engineers is R. H. McKim, *Thinking Visually: A Strategy Manual for Problem Solving* (Belmont, Calif.: Lifetime Learning Publications, 1980).
5. George Odiorne has written an excellent book that describes the troubles we have experienced because we can't manage change in modern society. He describes a system for introducing change in the light of all the forces that resist innovation and creativity. See *The Change Resisters: How They Prevent Progress and What Managers Can Do About Them* (Englewood Cliffs, N.J.: Prentice-Hall, 1981).

6. G. Polya, *How to Solve It* (Garden City, N.Y.: Doubleday & Company, 1957).

7. See M. Tushman and W. Moore, *Readings in the Management of Innovation* (Boston: Pitman Publishing, 1982) for a good collection of papers dealing with the problems associated with the management of innovation and some suggested alternative solutions.

9.

Making Decisions

The man who insists upon seeing with perfect clearness
before he decides, never decides.

FREDERIC AMIEL

From this chapter you will learn:

- *Why using a rational process is important in decision making*
- *What the basic steps are in a rational process of decision making*
- *What tools you can use to quantify important elements in the decision situation*
- *Which decisions should be made by groups, and how to increase the effectiveness of this method*

All managers have one central function in common. They must choose courses of action from among various competing alternatives, knowing that professional reputation is determined largely by the quality of decision making. Quite often, executives are evaluated by superiors, subordinates, and peers in terms of their *last few decisions*. Unfortunately, the effect of previous competent decisions decays rapidly, so that an executive's reputation is based upon most recent choices, whether they were correct or incorrect.

> *If a single characteristic is crucial to success as an administrator, it is the ability to make the correct decision when faced with imperfect information.*

Effective executives know they must concentrate on decision skills. A decision changes the direction of the organization. The degree of change may be major or minor, short term or long range, but the entire collection of decisions made (or avoided) by a single executive over a period of time can combine to influence even the largest enterprise in major ways. Human relations skills, long hours of work, and intense effort cannot overcome a series of incompetent decisions that limit the organization to making the best of a bad situation.

A basic assumption of this chapter is that the decision process can be described and, of greater importance, it can be learned. With diligent effort and a modicum of intelligence, any administrator can learn to be a better decision maker. *Capable decision makers are made, not born.* Unfortunately, the acquisition and improvement of decision-making skills is not easy. The critical factor is the actual application of the decision process in the real world by you, the reader. The combination of the correct approach and experience in using it in the real world will significantly improve the quality of your technical as well as managerial decisions. This chapter will introduce you to the correct approach to decision making.

*You can learn
to be a better
decision maker*

The Importance of Using a Process for Making Decisions

One traditional portrait of a successful executive is that of a rock-faced, dynamic individualist, his necktie at half-mast, a large cigar in the corner of his mouth, answering a battery of telephones that never stop ringing. He fires off instantaneous decisions, each involving millions of dollars and hundreds of people. All of this is done without hesitation and the decisions are invariably correct. Relying on hunches, intuition, guesses, an incredible memory, and unerring judgment, the executive amasses a great empire and then manages it perfectly while never moving from his great leather chair. All of this is fiction, of course. Today, in a world of international competition where technology expands exponentially and decisions are complicated by an abundance of data but a shortage of information, this traditional portrait is clearly out of date.

Successful executives have now replaced hunches and guesses with rational analysis of options, including quantification of end results, assessment of probabilities, and careful determination of strategy. The emphasis is now upon rational judgment and analysis of facts. The complex process of decision making has been broken apart into less complicated subcategories that comprise the decision process. This stepwise approach assists the executive in systematically determining appropriate goals, comparing the available alternatives in terms of probability, costs, benefits, and risks. Various actions or entire strategies may be compared in terms of goal achievement and additional options generated if those already examined are found inadequate. Using such a process makes decision making easier, more systematic, and more successful.

Using a rational decision-making process also makes it easier to sell decisions to others in the organization who are responsible for implementation or evaluation of the person proposing a particular course of action. The decision and the process used to reach the decision must be defensible to superiors, subordinates, and peers. What alternatives were available? What criteria were used? What order of importance was assumed? How was each alternative evaluated in terms of the criteria? How was a particular course of action singled out as best? Why? A haphazard, unexplainable decision will not survive these questions. "That seemed to be the best" is no defense. Only a rational decision process will do.

Rational analysis of options improves decision quality

We look next at a basic model of rational decision making, and then discuss two specific methods of applying it to make defensible decisions in different situations.

The Basic Decision Process Has Five Steps

In its simplest form, the correct approach to making a rational decision in any situation consists of five steps:

1. Definition of the problem.

2. Listing of options.

3. Definition of criteria.

4. Analysis of the options.

5. Choice of a course of action.

Let's briefly look at each of these steps in turn.

Definition of the problem. Decision making is oriented toward problem solving. Without identification and definition of the problem(s), no decision is possible, or, in fact, necessary. No problem, no decision. In order to define the existence of a problem there must be an individual or group of individuals who have the problem (the decision makers). These individuals must possess an objective. Call it a goal, a norm, a bogey, a yardstick, a standard, or an objective. In essence, it is a desired result. You will remember from Chapter 5 that a problem exists when a goal has been determined, actual results are known (or are estimable), a difference exists between the desired outcome and the actual outcome, and the difference is significant in the mind of the decision maker.

Listing of options. At least two courses of action must be available to the decision maker, and they must be unequal in ability to achieve the goal (in removal of the significant difference between desired and actual outcomes). If only one possible course of action exists, the manager may still have a problem, but there is no decision to make. Similarly, if more than one course of action exists, but the final result is the same regardless of the action chosen, there is no decision to make.

In many cases, the number of options that exist is far greater than is obvious. Search for these not-so-obvious courses of action is a critical part of decision making. If the optimal option is not included in the list of alternatives examined, the decision made will necessarily be suboptimal. What are the alternatives? Can we combine? Simplify? Create others? Have all possible courses of action been included? This mode of thought, of course, involves creative, imaginative thinking, and is very hard work. A basic human trait is to limit search and get right to the business at hand. "Once a problem is identified, we must be decisive and choose a course of action." Many opportunities for optimal decisions are foregone by this type of thinking.

Definition of criteria. What, specifically, are the objectives of the individual? Maximization of expected gain in the form of future profits might be one of them. Some measure of expected utility may be more appropriate. Perhaps minimizing costs, discomfort, pain, or even losses in combat might be of paramount importance. Some goals cannot be measured directly in terms of monetary gain or loss. Goal determination is difficult even when only one objective is considered. An additional complication is added when more than one goal is involved. Subjective weights must be attached to each goal in order of importance. The decision maker always attaches these weights, either explicitly or implicitly, because if no differing weights are assigned to the objectives, the weights are of necessity equal. Magnitude of importance cannot be avoided if more than one

The five basic steps of rational decision making

goal is sought. The problem solver must ask himself or herself specifically what goals must be achieved and what order of relative importance must exist.

Analysis of the options. Each possible course of action must now be carefully studied in terms of desired outcomes, that is, how well the options will likely attain the objectives and remove the difference between desired and actual output. This involves computation, estimation, and comparison. Information must be gathered and facts carefully separated from opinion. The reliability of information sources must be assessed objectively. Risks must be examined and quantified. Then, various alternatives can be analyzed in terms of goal achievement and ranked in order of desirability. The inevitable tradeoffs can then be analyzed. After all of this, a state of doubt may still exist as to which choice is best; however, that doubt is now out in the open and subject to rational discussion and attack.

Choice of a course of action. A decision is made when a particular course of action is chosen from among those available. Whether the problem has been solved depends upon whether or not the alternative chosen was "best" and whether or not resolution of the problem was within the control of the decision maker. If he or she has chosen the optimal alternative available to him or her and the undesirable discrepancy between goal and actual performance still exists, the problem may be insoluble. Otherwise, when the course of action is chosen and implemented the difference disappears, the goal is achieved, and the problem solved.

Although all decision processes are based on these five steps, they vary in the methods used to quantify benefits, risks, probability and desirability of certain outcomes, and so on. During the past two decades a new technique for quantifying factors has emerged that may be applied to virtually any decision problem. This approach, called *decision analysis,* has been applied with great success in many kinds of situations. Several authors have argued that this technique will be to managers of the '80s as the hand-held calculator is to scientists and engineers.

Quantifying factors by "decision analysis"

The objective of decision analysis is to add a logical structure to any decision situation so that subjective assessments are brought into the open and complex decisions are reduced to a series of simpler subdecisions. One form of decision analysis can be applied in situations where only one criterion must be met (for example, maximization of profit), and another form is suitable for situations where multiple criteria must be considered (multicriteria decision analysis).

You'll find an overview and an example of each form here, though it's beyond the scope of this book to go into either in depth. If you wish to learn more about the application of these methods, consult the books suggested in the "Further Readings" section at the end of this chapter.

Making Decisions Based on a Single Criterion

Decision analysis is applied to situations involving only a single criterion by breaking down the second, third, and fourth steps of the basic decision process into these seven substeps:

1. Enumeration of the available *acts* open to the decision maker (an act is something the decision maker is able to control).

The steps of single criterion decision analysis

2. Consideration of the possible states of nature or *events* the decision maker is subject to.

3. Assignment of *conditional values* to each combination of act and event (the result if a particular act is chosen and a specific event occurs).

4. Selection of a *weight* for each event (the probability of occurrence).

5. Calculation of a *weighted average* of the conditional values for each act (expected profit, cost, or utility).

6. Selection of maximization or minimization of this weighted average as a decision criterion.

7. Consideration of other noneconomic consequences in a well-structured search for the optimal strategy.

As an example of this approach, assume you are an executive in a small oil company with limited financial resources. A particular piece of land owned by the firm may or may not contain petroleum. A competitor has offered to lease the land for a total price of $100,000. This offer will expire within one week. If you accept the lease opportunity, your company will receive a certain payment of $100,000. If you decide to refuse the lease, you are then faced with a decision concerning drilling. If your firm drills for oil, the drilling expense will be $300,000. Four outcomes are possible: (1) dry hole, (2) natural gas, (3) natural gas with some oil, or (4) oil. Historical data yield the information listed in Table 9-1 for fifty similar pieces of land where drilling was performed. If a dry hole is found, your firm will not be able to lease the land since other firms will not be interested in drilling where your firm was unsuccessful in locating petroleum. Ignoring tax considerations, reliability of estimates, personal risk if you make an error, and assuming that your firm will not be bankrupted by a loss of $300,000 for unsuccessful drilling, what is your decision?

A picture of this decision situation is shown in Figure 9-1, in the form of a *decision tree*. The numbers on the four branches of the tree following point C are probabilities. They are computed by dividing the number of times a structure occurred by the total number of trials (for example, dry holes occurred 10 times out of 50 trials and 10/50 equals 0.2).

Construct a decision tree

Solution of the problem involves working backward through the tree from right to left. If one were to arrive at point C many times, what would be the long-term average profit per arrival? This is termed the *expected value* of point C. Basically, it represents a weighted average of the possible values of profit, the weights being the probability that a particular value of profit will occur. Each decision to lease would bring the manager to point A, and each such arrival would result in $100,000 for certain. Similarly, each arrival at point B would result in a certain profit of zero. Each decision that causes the administrator to arrive at point C would result in uncertain profits. The possible values are −$300,000; $0; $300,000; or $900,000. The weighted average or expectation can be computed when one realizes that the probabilities represent chances of receiving each of the end-value profits. This expected value would be

Table 9-1. Data on Similar Pieces of Land.

Resulting Structure	Number of Times Occurred	Estimated Value of Structure
Dry hole	10	0
Natural gas	20	$ 300,000
Gas and oil	15	$ 600,000
Oil	5	$1,200,000
Total	50	

First Decision	Second Decision	Resulting Structure	Final Profit ($1000s)

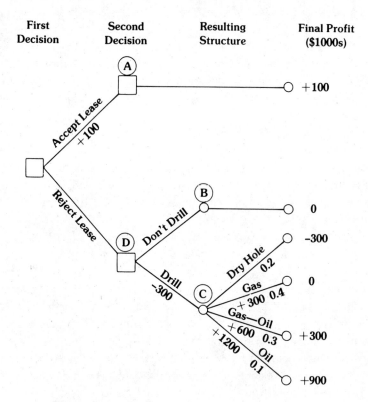

Figure 9-1. Decision tree for leasing decision.

$0.2(-300,000) + 0.4(0) + 0.3(+300,000) + 0.1(+900,000) = -60,000 + 0 + 90,000 + 90,000 = \$ +120,000.$

A modified tree can now be constructed in which the expected value of arriving at a particular point is represented by the number in the square at that point (Figure 9-2). The decision maker can choose to proceed to point A for $\$+100,000$, to point D and then B for $0, or to point D and then C for $\$+120,000$. In this case, an expected profit is assumed to be equivalent to a certain profit of the same amount. Since the last figure ($120,000) is the highest profit attainable in this situation, the optimal strategy would be to reject the lease and drill. The possible outcomes and their probabilities are listed in Table 9-2.

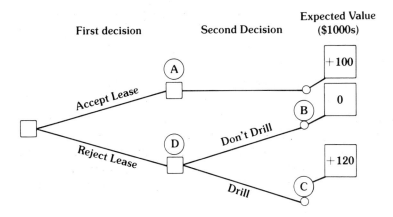

Figure 9-2. Modified tree for leasing decision.

Suppose, however, that an experiment or test can be performed that will provide additional information. The experiment costs $20,000 and will indicate the general category (alpha, beta, or delta) of underground structure that is present. For the same fifty previous observations the results of tests performed are given in Table 9-3.

Since you have decided to drill, would you also recommend that the test be performed? Can the value of information derived from the test possibly be worth $20,000? Again, a diagram of the problem is helpful (Figure 9-3). Probabilities for test results and for resulting structure are computed from the historical data presented in Table 9-3.

Modify the tree to include new information

Table 9-2. Possible Outcomes.

Outcome	Probability
$300,000 loss	0.2
Break even	0.4
$300,000 gain	0.3
$900,000 gain	0.1

Table 9-3. Data on Similar Pieces of Land.

ACTUAL RESULT AFTER DRILLING	CATEGORY OF STRUCTURE INDICATED BY THE TEST			TOTAL
	Alpha	Beta	Delta	
Dry hole	10	0	0	10
Natural gas	10	10	0	20
Gas and oil	0	10	5	15
Oil	0	0	5	5
Total	20	20	10	50

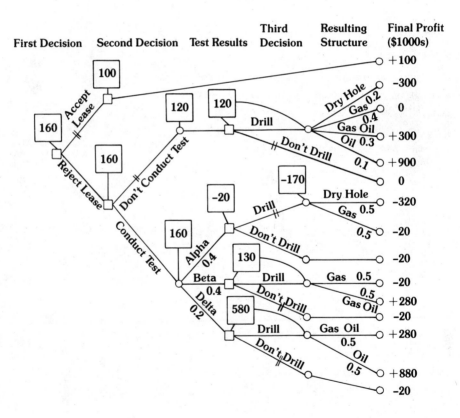

Figure 9-3. Modified tree for test decision.

For example, an alpha category occurred 20 times in 50 tests (20/50 = 0.4) and when an alpha category occurred, dry holes occurred 10 times (10/20 = 0.5). Study this diagram carefully before proceeding further.

Solution of the problem is conducted as before, by backward induction from right to left. Whenever an event fork is reached, the outcomes of all possible events are multiplied by their associated probability of occurrence and summed for all values. This expected value is assumed to be equivalent to a certain value of the same amount. Whenever a decision must be made, inferior decisions in terms of expected values (or certain amounts) are ruled out with double lines(//). Appropriate values are placed in the squares at every branch of the tree and are carried along for further comparison at branches to the left. The optimal strategy consists of all decisions not ruled out when the origin at the left edge of the tree is reached.

Determine the optimal strategy

The optimal strategy is now fully determined: Reject the lease. Conduct the test. If alpha ... don't drill. If beta ... drill. If delta ... drill. How can the decision maker emerge from the right-hand terminal points of the tree if this strategy is invoked? Five ways exist and are shown in Table 9-4. You should verify that there is no other combination of decisions in this problem that will yield a higher expected profit.

Note that without the test the firm should drill, with a resultant long-term profit expectation of $120,000 as compared to the $160,000 shown in the tree. Spending $20,000 for more information and then acting on the basis of that information increases profits by $40,000 after the test is paid for. Perhaps of greater import is

Table 9-4. Possible Outcomes.

Path	Resulting Structure	Final Profit	Probability
Reject; conduct; alpha; don't	Unknown	$20,000 loss	0.4
Reject; conduct; beta; drill	Gas	$20,000 loss	0.2 = (0.4 × 0.5)
	Gas + oil	$280,000 gain	0.2 = (0.4 × 0.5)
Reject; conduct; delta; drill	Gas + oil	$280,000 gain	0.1 = (0.2 × 0.5)
	Oil	$880,000 gain	0.1 = (0.2 × 0.5)

the fact that with the above strategy the firm will lose a maximum of $20,000. Without the test the firm could lose as much as $300,000! Using the test information intelligently, the firm might repeat this decision as many as fifteen times and lose on them all for the same total loss as a single drilling decision without test information if a dry hole is the result.

Dealing with Uncertainty

The oil drilling example above involved many estimates. What is the probability in the real world that oil will be worth exactly $1,200,000 or that drilling will cost exactly $300,000? Very small indeed. What if we did not have extensive historical data about similar pieces of property on which to base our estimates? Decision analysis deals with uncertainties like these and errors of assessment by use of sensitivity analysis.

Sensitivity analysis in decision theory is broadly defined as the careful study of the responsiveness of conclusions to changes or errors in parameter values and assumptions. Some decisions are sensitive to minor changes in the values of costs, profits, probabilities, and so on. The optimal decision is easily moved. In other cases the optimal decision remains unchanged despite major changes in inputs. No thorough, rational decision analysis is complete without explicit examination of such sensitivities.

Sensitivity analysis determines which factors must be assessed precisely

The usual approach is to hold all aspects of the model constant and vary each parameter while observing the influence of the changes upon the optimal decision. If a parameter may be varied over the full range of conceivable values with no change in optimal decision, the decision is not sensitive to that particular parameter, and no resources should be expended to determine a more exact value for it. When the decision *is* sensitive to changes that are within the realm of possibility, more precision is required and further information must be obtained. At that point, the decision maker must examine the benefits of additional information compared to the costs of obtaining it.

Suppose the probabilities of certain events cannot be derived from the relative frequencies of past occurrences in similar situations. If the decision maker is not comfortable with subjectively assessing these probabilities, different questions are asked: "How far can my analysis continue before I must assess probabilities, and what are their critical values? Are there obviously inferior branches in the tree that may be eliminated immediately? At what point would acts be equally desirable?" Subjective probabilities are then introduced as a final step where needed to isolate an optimal strategy.

Consider this example of the decision analysis approach using sensitivity analysis. The acting dean of a business college was visited by the head custodian, who announced that the master key had been stolen from his office. The key would open any door in all three buildings in the college complex. Every classroom, faculty, and administrative office, the library, the computation center, and so on, could be entered by someone with the pass key. The custodian stated that he had used the key during the previous night shift, had placed it on a small hook on the wall inside his closet door, but had found it missing that morning.

The problem was serious for the dean because valuable equipment and confidential academic materials such as teacher's manuals and examinations were now vulnerable. His first act was to telephone the college security office, inform them of the missing key, and request that additional watchmen be sent to the college. He suggested that their rounds be made more random (as opposed to regularly scheduled) and that they watch carefully for any unusual activities or people, especially during the nights and weekends. Next, he informed the faculty and staff of the loss so that valuables might be locked in desks or cabinets or removed from the complex. All academic materials were to be placed in the dean's safe or under lock and key.

A real problem solved using the decision process with sensitivity analysis

The next decision was whether the lock cylinders should be changed so the master key would no longer work. A locksmith visited the college. He felt that all the cylinders could be changed within eight days after a firm order was placed by the dean. The cylinders would have to be shipped air freight from Los Angeles and every trained locksmith put to work on the project. Estimated costs would be $12,000. The cost for an individual lock to be changed would be about $60 if done on a rush basis, including the cost of freight, cylinder, installation, and new keys. The dean realized that he could change all the locks, none of the locks, or any number of locks in between these two extremes. For ease of analysis he limited these acts to three options: (1) change all the locks ($12,000); (2)

change the critical locks, including the library, computation center, and dean's office ($3600); or (3) change none of the locks ($0).

Three events seemed possible. The master key might have been stolen for monetary purposes. Electric typewriters, calculators, radios, and so on, were housed in various rooms in the complex. The key might have been stolen for academic purposes, such as to obtain quizzes, examinations, and roll books. The possibility existed that the key was not stolen at all but was lost. There were no special markings on the key, so there would be no way of knowing it was a master key. Careful analysis of the offices and classrooms led the dean to estimate the following possible losses: (1) Given current precautions, the replacement cost of equipment that could reasonably be removed from all offices was about $10,000; (2) if the locks were changed on critical offices before the key could be used, these would be protected, and the monetary value of equipment in rooms that could still be opened by the master key amounted to about $2500; (3) the monetary value of unprotected academic material was assessed at $0. This third assumption is not critical to the analysis. If the dean had cared whether or not these materials were stolen, he could have asked, "What dollar amount would I be willing to pay to avoid losing these items?" This monetary equivalent could then have been added to the appropriate terminal values.

With this information at hand, the dean sketched Figure 9-4. Realizing that some possibilities were being ignored (such as being "hit" for monetary purposes more than once or the thief's being caught by Security), the dean simplified the diagram to Figure 9-5. Since the total cost would be $12,000 if all locks were changed, the various events on the top branch were reduced to a certain single cost of $12,000. The two events "stolen academic" and "lost" were combined, since they would yield the same incremental cost of $0 and $3600.

The decision is simplified

A striking fact became apparent. "Change all" the locks was dominated by each of the other two acts. Regardless of which event occurred, the cost of "change all" was higher than any possible values for "change some" or "change none." It did not make sense to spend a sure $12,000 to protect the college from a maximum possible loss of $10,000. Thus, this inferior alternative was eliminated from the analysis.

The choice now depended upon the probability that the key was stolen for monetary purposes (p) versus the probability that it was stolen for academic purposes or lost ($1-p$). If the value of p

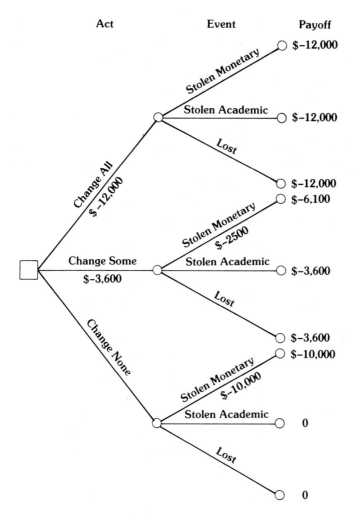

| Act | Event | Payoff |

Change All $-12,000
- Stolen Monetary → $-12,000
- Stolen Academic → $-12,000
- Lost → $-12,000

Change Some $-3,600
- Stolen Monetary $-2500 → $-6,100
- Stolen Academic → $-3,600
- Lost → $-3,600

Change None
- Stolen Monetary $-10,000 → $-10,000
- Stolen Academic → 0
- Lost → 0

Figure 9-4. Decision tree for lock decision.

were zero, $(1-p)$ would equal 1. The better act would be to change none, since a cost of 0 is preferable to a cost of $3600. As the value of p increases, the act "change none" becomes more costly, until a point is reached where the two acts are equally undesirable. For values of p above this point of indifference up to $p = 1$, the act

What does the probability have to be?

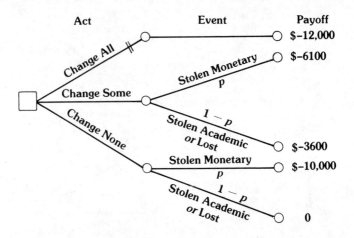

Figure 9-5. Modified tree for lock decision.

"change some" becomes less costly. The point of indifference occurs when the expected cost of "change some" equals that of "change none":

$$6100p + 3600(1-p) = 10{,}000p + 0(1-p)$$
$$6100p + 3600 - 3600p = 10{,}000p$$
$$3600 = p(10{,}000 - 6100 + 3600)$$
$$3600 = p(7500)$$
$$\frac{3600}{7500} = p = 0.48$$

If the probability that the key was stolen for monetary purposes equals 0.48 and the probability that it was stolen for academic purposes or lost equals 0.52, the expected cost for "change some" would be 0.48(6100) + 0.52(3600) = 2928 + 1872 = 4800. The expected cost of "change none" would be 0.48(10,000) + 0.52(0) = 4800. The dean was quite willing to make the decision on the basis of expected costs since the amounts involved were not critical to management of the college.

He realized that expenditure of time and effort to assess a precise value of p might not be necessary. If p were clearly greater than, say, 50 percent, he should change some of the locks. If p were clearly smaller than this value, he would change none of them. If p were in the vicinity of 50 percent, the decision would be more diffi-cult and some refinement of the assessment would be appropriate. With this in mind, he asked the custodian to provide more details. In the course of the discussion, the custodian stated that he had returned to the college in the morning, unlocked his closet door, and found the key missing. The dean wondered how the key could be removed from a locked closet unless the thief already had a closet key but not a master key, an unlikely combination of events. Under further questioning, the custodian admitted that he could not in fact remember hanging the key on the hook in his closet, al-though this was his usual practice. He was certain, however, that his door was locked when he returned in the morning.

The dean was thus led to assess the probability that the key was lost to be rather high. There was some chance that the custo-dian had left his door open during the night and the thief had re-moved the master key and then locked the door with it, but that seemed unlikely. With the additional information provided by the custodian, the dean assessed the probability that the key was stolen for monetary purposes to be considerably less than 0.5, so he made the decision to change none of the locks.

The choice is made

In a similar circumstance, the dean of a school of engineering in a Big Ten university chose the opposite act and replaced all the locks at a cost of $16,000. Perhaps in that instance he was correct. In the example above, the decision was apparently correct because the key was never used for either academic purposes or equipment theft to the best of my knowledge. I made the decision in Septem-ber 1969.

Making Decisions Based on Multiple Criteria

The previous section introduced a process for making decisions on the basis of a single criterion (monetary value). In many situa-tions using only one measure of effectiveness is appropriate. To the extent that you are able to reduce the total effects of a decision to a single measure, it is clearly worthwhile for you to do so. However, in many complex situations this is not possible, and you must ex-plicitly define a finite set of goals and weight them accordingly. The steps for making a decision based on multiple criteria follow very closely the basic process introduced earlier. They are:

1. Definition of the problem.

The steps of multicriteria decision analysis

2. Listing of the alternatives.
3. Definition of criteria.
4. Assigning of weights to criteria.
5. Evaluation of each alternative for all criteria.
6. Choice of a course of action.

The following example illustrates this multicriteria approach to decision analysis.

Three aerospace companies were asked to submit a proposal to the Department of Defense for an advanced solid-fueled injection rocket for the Advent missile. The federal government designated Space Technology Laboratories (STL) as their contracting agent in this program. The project required major scientific advances, because such a project had never been undertaken before. For this and many other reasons, STL could not reduce all factors to a single monetary value and rate the three proposals in terms of mathematical expectations of cost or profit.

Eventually, five criteria were specified by STL, who was to decide which firm received the contract:

1. *Understanding the problem.* Does the firm realize the potential difficulties involved? Is it clearly recognized that the project will involve a significant advancement in the state-of-the-art?

2. *Technical approach.* Is the suggested scientific/engineering solution of the problem feasible? Is it optimal? Even if it will work, can this firm do it?

3. *Cost.* How much will the proposal cost the government? Is the cost projection accurate? Are all costs included? What is the probability of a cost overrun?

4. *Cost effectiveness.* What are the tradeoffs? What would we give up in performance for lower costs? What are we getting in specific measures of performance for various cost figures? Has the firm analyzed and presented these tradeoffs to us? Are they credible?

5. *Capability to meet schedule.* Can this firm deliver the product at the right time and place so that the entire Advent project will not be held up?

Clearly, it would be difficult to reduce all these criteria to monetary values. For example, how much is "understanding the problem" worth in cost dollars? More importantly, if each criterion cannot be expressed in some common basis, how may the three firms be evaluated and compared?

The next step to be taken by STL was definition of a scoring mechanism. Each criterion was agreed to be worth a maximum of 100 points and a minimum of 0. Zero was considered "totally unsatisfactory." For example, a proposal that contained no cost/effectiveness analysis of potential tradeoffs would receive a zero. A score of 100 meant that the criterion was satisfied completely, to the maximum possible degree. An intermediate score of, say, 50 would be interpreted as "adequate," that is, acceptable but certainly not outstanding or even completely satisfactory.

Each of the five criteria were then weighted in order of importance. If they had not been weighted explicitly, they were of necessity considered equal in importance, and this is itself an implicit weighting. The issue is unavoidable. The question "What is the relative order of importance and by how much?" had to be dealt with. In this particular case, STL decided upon the values listed in Table 9-5. Technical approach and cost were considered most important. Cost effectiveness and problem understanding were important enough to include as criteria, but, of those considered, they were least important. The other criterion was of intermediate importance. The absolute magnitude of the numbers is irrelevant. Only the *relative* values are of concern.

The three firms, Aerojack, Theobald, and Herculax, were given three months to prepare a written proposal and submit it to STL. Two weeks after the written reports were due, a presentation

Table 9-5. Assigning of Weights to Criteria.

Criterion	Relative Weight
Understanding the problem	3
Technical approach	5
Cost	5
Cost effectiveness	3
Capability to meet schedule	4

Table 9-6. Evaluation of Each Alternative for Each Criterion.

			STL'S SCORING	
Criterion	Weight	Aerojack	Theobald	Herculax
Understanding the problem	3	25	75	100
Technical approach	5	0	75	100
Cost	5	100	75	25
Cost effectiveness	3	100	75	0
Capability to meet schedule	4	50	80	100

Weight the criteria and score each alternative

to STL management of the salient points and discussion of the proposal were to be conducted by each firm. On the basis of the written proposal and the personal presentation, STL rated the proposals as given in Table 9-6. STL then computed a weighted total score for each firm by multiplying each weight by the firm's scores and summing for each firm. Aerojack achieved 1075 total points [(3 × 25) + (5 × 0) + (5 × 100) + (3 × 100) + (4 × 50) — 1075]. Similarly, Theobald received 1520 points and Herculax received 1325. The contract was awarded to Theobald.

The important elements of multicriteria decision making are contained in this aerospace example. As a *minimum*, STL was forced to take certain definite steps in the contract-awarding process. Complex decisions involve complicated and, perhaps, competing interests. The decision had to be defended to the Department of Defense, in this case the superior of STL. The two losing firms had a right to know the basis for rejection of their proposals. For self-preservation and industry-wide reputation, the management of STL was forced to make explicit and defend the basis of the contract decision. This meant that each step in the award process had to be open and rational.

In this multicriteria process, ranking and assigning weights to criteria are especially important. It is sometimes useful to classify criteria as either *musts* or *wants*.[1] *Musts* define the restraints that are inviolable. Some objectives are so critical in the mind of the decision maker that any act that does not yield a particular result is immediately inadmissible. These impossible options are removed from the analysis at the beginning. This makes search for the optimal act much more efficient by constraining the search to a limited set of possibilities for future analysis. Criteria that are *wants* allow us to order the relative desirability of the alternatives that remain after *musts* have been considered. *Wants* allow us to estimate pros and cons, advantages and disadvantages, to further refine our search.

*Separate the musts **from the** wants **and the** ignorables*

Perhaps a third category of criteria ought to be introduced — the *ignorables*. An analysis can be taken too far in terms of search, time and effort, money expended, and objectives considered. The wise manager will decide as part of the analysis which objectives are of minor importance and safely ignorable. Attention is thus confined to the *musts* and *wants*.

Multicriteria decision analysis has proven to be successful in real world projects such as airport location and weapons system design. With situations of this complexity, expert consultants, healthy budgets, long lead times, and sophisticated computer hardware and software are usually required. The typical engineering manager does not ordinarily have access to all of these resources. Nevertheless, for projects of moderate complexity, the basic approach outlined in this chapter *is* available and its proper use will improve the quality of decisions significantly.

Group Decision Making Can Be Effective

Committees and other formal, small groups are important components of the participative management style advocated in this book. This is especially true in problem solving and decision making. It should be noted at the outset that group decision making is cumbersome when compared to that of the individual manager. It takes more time and generally does not produce results equal to that of the *best* individual decision maker. However, solutions and decisions arrived at by a small group, after deliberation and discussion, are better than the average decisions of individuals in the group when

- The problem is technical rather than attitudinal.
- The initial judgments of the individuals are not identical (there is a wide range of potential solutions).
- The task can be subdivided into smaller assignments.

119

- Rewards for solution can be given to the entire group rather than individuals within the group.
- The task includes potential traps that individuals might miss.
- The project requires expertise in more than one area.

At times, the quality of the group decision is better than that of any individual decision because of the effects of synergy. And research has shown the occurrence of what is called the risky shift, a propensity for a group to choose a more risk-taking position than the riskiest individual would take because the responsibility can be spread among all group members if the decision results in failure.

Group decision making can lead to better quality and acceptance

In addition to the quality of the solution, group decision making has other advantages. Members will understand the decision better and they will be more likely to accept it and thus improve its implementation. Active discussion by the group to determine common goals, choose work methods, modify operations, or solve similar problems is more effective than is separate instruction of individual members, or imposition of new procedures by superior authority. Motivation and support for the change are increased if the individuals involved participate in formulation of the changes.

There do exist certain liabilities in the group approach in addition to the time involved. Pressure from group members may lead to conformity; thus, agreement becomes more important than finding the best solution. This promotes a tendency to satisfice rather than maximize. Also, certain strong individuals may tend to dominate the group and overly influence the deliberations and decision. Conflict may be created if individuals feel strongly about certain points that are then rejected by others in the group.

Whether or not the group approach is appropriate depends upon several important criteria. Is speed essential? Is there an individual whose outstanding skills would be diluted by the group? Is the decision so unimportant that the time and expense of the group approach cannot be justified and, in fact, the group would be insulted by the assignment? Have you already made up your mind so you will be reluctant to change even if the group decides otherwise? If the answer to any one of these questions is yes, then a group approach should be avoided.

As a manager, you must be certain in your own mind and communicate to the group at the outset just what authority is being given. Will the group submit a carefully thought-out analysis of the problem? Will it prepare a list of advantages and disadvantages and potential solutions? Will it recommend a specific course of action? Or will it be responsible for the decision and its implementation? If you do not make your position absolutely clear at the beginning of the assignment, you are asking for trouble!

If you have decided to use the group approach and have determined the level of authority to be delegated, follow these principles in dealing with the group:

- Inform the members of their authority, what is expected of them, and set a target date for completion. Do this face-to-face and then commit it to writing for their personal files.

- Help the members get acquainted — make certain they have been introduced and know something of each other's background and qualifications.

- Emphasize search for options, listening, and the honest exchange of opinions.

- Avoid premature judgment and the selling of personal opinions (do not push a predetermined solution).

- Do not permit a single member to dominate discussion (use every member of the group).

- Keep the discussion level energetic and alert by maintaining intensity and personal interest.

- At the end of every meeting, make certain everyone knows what has been accomplished, what remains to be done, by whom, and when.

Follow these principles for deciding with a group

Some Final Observations About Decision Making

Regardless of which rational process you use in a real decision situation, you should strive to meet the following guidelines.

Definitions should be crystal clear. Ambiguity and uncertainty in meaning should be eliminated. For example, your goals as a decision maker should be defined in nonambiguous dimensions and values. "Maximum happiness" is too ambiguous and vague to serve as a goal.

The decision process should be communicable. One of the tests of rationality in decision making is the ability of the decision maker to verbalize or describe the process used in choosing a course of action. This includes *why* as well as *how*.

Collection of data should be unbiased. All sources should be treated with objectivity. Discarding of information should be justified. The decision maker should include all available facts in the analysis of alternatives, criteria, and outcomes, regardless of personal bias or prejudice.

The decision process should be reproducible. Different decision makers might assess different probabilities given the same facts and might have differing attitudes toward risk. If so, they might not make the same decision. But in the absence of these differences, another decision maker faced with identical information, options, and goals should be led to the same course of action.

Opinions should not be treated as facts. Every effort should be made to isolate reality from beliefs, judgments, views, and speculation. Moreover, information should always be evaluated in terms of the reliability of its source.

Choice of action should be the final step. A common characteristic of incompetent or mediocre administrators is reversal of the decision process. An act is chosen and then facts, opinions, options, and goals are manipulated in order to justify the choice. Not only does this result in poor decisions, it is the primary characteristic of the uneducated intellect.

To the extent that you are able to meet these guidelines, your decisions will be improved.

Once you have isolated the alternative to be implemented, but before you have made the decision irrevocably, it is wise to assess the *undesirable* consequences that might occur if the decision is implemented. Where are the potential pitfalls? What are the reasons, valid or not, mitigating against success? Are there sufficient dangers for your department, your firm, or you that a safer second-best option should be chosen instead? Not all these hazards will have been brought to light and analyzed exhaustively in the decision process. A competent, secure manager will not only be able to tolerate this type of criticism but will welcome it. Admittedly, the criticism is more welcome before rather than after the decision has been made.

Your decision may "satisfice," not optimize

You should realize that realistically, it is not possible to optimize your entire "universe." You may end up *satisficing,* a term originated by Herbert Simon. In studying many decisions and the process used by numerous decision makers, Simon theorized that the goal of decision making is not, in fact, optimization. Decisions that suffice or satisfy some appropriate but arbitrary level of effectiveness are chosen. Indefinite search for *the* single optimal alternative is not usually undertaken. If a minimum hurdle rate is achieved, that is deemed sufficient, and further search is abandoned. This is understandable. Search costs money and time. Unlimited search for a single best alternative in many cases cannot be justified in terms of the incremental value of the search relative to the incremental cost. Also, it is possible that satisficing at one level of the system is, in fact, optimizing at another level. The president of a corporation may allocate limited funds to research and development because that action will free more funds for advertising and production.

Whether or not a decision is "good" depends upon the process used to reach it considering the information available to the decision maker. A "correct" decision must be judged in terms of the final outcome of the decision. At times, a "good" decision may not be a "correct" decision once the final outcome is known. A poker player who draws to an inside straight and receives the card he needs will have made a correct decision but not a good one. Over the long term, choices of this sort will not lead to satisfactory outcomes. A desirable final result, then, cannot invariably be related to good decision making or undesirable results traced to bad decisions.

Finally, the decision should be clearly communicated to those responsible for implementation. This is done best through face-to-face contact with follow-up documentation kept on hand by all parties. A control mechanism must also be set up assuring you that what was intended is what was actually implemented. Some specific target date should be established so that the actual results of the decision may be compared against the desired outcomes. This provides excellent feedback, a control mechanism, and also furnishes information for future decisions that may be necessary in solving similar problems.

Summary

- Capable decision makers are made, not born. Decision-making skills can be learned.
- Using a rational process makes decision making easier, more systematic, and more certain, and renders the decision more easily defensible.

- Basic steps of rational decision making include definition of the problem, listing of options, definition of criteria, analysis of the alternatives, and choice of action.
- Single criterion and multicriteria decision analysis provide tools for quantifying basic elements and for analyzing options in the decision situation.
- Group decision making offers certain advantages but must be done thoughtfully, following certain specific principles.
- There is no guarantee that a good decision will end up being correct.

Note

1. The "must/want" approach outlined in this chapter was introduced by Kepner and Tregoe. An excellent source for the reader interested in expansion and elaboration of this approach is C. H. Kepner & B. B. Tregoe, *The Rational Manager* (New York: McGraw-Hill, 1965).

Further Readings

1. D. R. Anderson, D. J. Sweeney, and T. A. Williams, *Quantitative Methods for Business*, Second Edition (St. Paul: West Publishing Company, 1983). This is a well-done, comprehensive coverage of mathematical approaches to certain management problems. It includes chapters on linear programming, inventory theory, network analysis, simulation, etc.

2. For a detailed coverage of decision analysis, see B. F. Baird, *Introduction to Decision Analysis* (North Scituate, Mass.: Duxbury Press, 1978). This work includes chapters on probability theory, the construction of decision diagrams, utility theory, sensitivity analysis, probability assessment, and multicriteria decision making. Much of the material in this chapter is taken from this work.

3. The following elaborate on the decision models of this chapter: A. Easton, *Complex Managerial Decisions Involving Multiple Objectives* (New York: John Wiley & Sons, 1973); R. Keeney and H. Raiffa, *Decisions with Multiple Objectives: Preferences and Value Trade-offs* (New York: John Wiley & Sons, 1976).

4. A more descriptive work on decision making is G. P. Huber, *Managerial Decision Making* (Glenview, Ill.: Scott, Foresman & Company, 1980). It includes chapters on group decision making, how to decide when to decide, and improving decisions involving multiple goals.

5. In a recent work, T. Saaty describes his "analytical hierarchy process" for improving decisions. The emphasis is on priorities, benefits/costs, and allocation of resources. See *Decision Making for Leaders: The Analytical Hierarchy Process for Decisions in a Complex World* (Belmont, Calif.: Lifetime Learning Publications, 1982).

10.

Understanding Your Organization

*What's the use of inventing a better system as long as
there just aren't enough folks with sense to go around!*

DOROTHY CANFIELD FISHER

From this chapter you will learn:

- *What the difference is between functional, project, and matrix
  forms of organization*
- *Why your top management might choose one or the other of
  these forms*
- *What problems you might experience in the project form of
  organization*
- *How a successful project manager gets the job done*

All of us work in some type of organization, a group of people
joined together formally for the purpose of achieving specific objectives. Different organizations have very different structures. Some
have a rigid design and a high degree of centralization. Others are
informal and decentralized. Still others have combinations of these
characteristics depending upon which part of the organization is
considered. As a new manager, you are subject to the structure of
the organization in which you work, but you have some influence
upon the nature of your unit of the organization and how it may

best achieve its objectives. Decisions you make regarding results, feedback mechanisms, the control process, and the degree of personal freedom allowed are all influenced by organization structure.

You will be a better manager if you understand the rationale behind your organization's structure. Furthermore, you will likely be responsible for major organizational decisions as you progress upward into middle and top management. It is not too early in your career to begin a critical evaluation of your organization's overall structure as well as the structure of your individual suborganization. The objective of this chapter is to assist you in this evaluation.

There Are Three Basic Organizational Structures

The functional organization concentrates on functional goals

The three basic forms of organization are the functional form, the project form, and the matrix form. The *functional* form is the traditional bureaucracy, characterized ideally by specialization of labor, fair promotions, rational authority, and logical goals. Its shape resembles a pyramid. Specialists are grouped by function and the dominant groups are sales, manufacturing, finance, and so on. This form of organization is shown in Figure 10-1.[1]

This model is based upon a continuous production of goods and services with well-defined similarity in functional groupings. The origin of this style is with religious, military, and nobility approaches. The underlying assumption is that we can design the organization like a machine and presume it will operate with efficiency, cranking out products and services, manned by efficient and productive workers with high morale.

The functional organization is a dichotomy composed of two classes of employees: line and staff. Line makes the decisions, possesses the authority, and commands the subgroups. Staff provides counsel and advice, does the thinking and most of the planning, but has no authority except as it influences the judgment of the line. Specialized offices that differ in objective from the main concern of the firm (for example, personnel) are staff in nature.

If a complex, one-time project occurs, accomplishment of the mission objectives may be impeded by the functional design, for the following reasons:

128

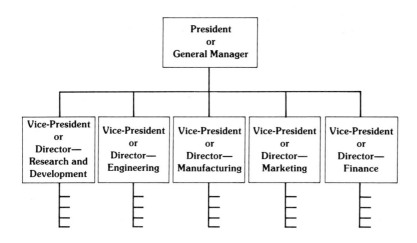

Figure 10-1. A functional organization.

- The *overall perspective* of the project is lost in the functional organization. The departments are concerned with only their part of the project without concern for the impact of their actions upon the entire program.

- No single manager is responsible for *total project costs.* Functional executives are concerned about only their specialized tasks and their portion of the budget.

- Many *skills are duplicated* in various departments thus causing competitive conflict and increasing costs.

- *Fast decision making is often required* in complex projects. Functional organizations must filter the decisions by passing them through all levels, thus causing delays while spreading the risk.

- Functional departments are accustomed to repetitive operations and *lack the flexibility* necessary to respond to changing project requirements.

- The traditional philosophy based upon vertical flow of power does not recognize *the importance of the horizontal and diagonal interactions necessary to get the job done.*

Potential hazards in the functional organization

These factors are so critical that unless someone concentrates upon *project* goals rather than traditional production or marketing goals, vast resources will be consumed before it is found that the project is already out of control. For all these reasons and more, the project and matrix approaches have been found to be advantageous for the management of large, special missions such as development of a new product, construction of a mass transit system or factory or dam, or administration of any major departure from "business as usual." It might be argued that more scientists and engineers work today in the project and matrix forms of organization than in the functional form. At least, the trend is certainly in this direction.

Project and matrix organizations concentrate on project goals

In the *project* form of organization, shown in Figure 10-2, personnel are relocated from their functional slots to positions subordinate to a project manager. These relocations are formal but last only for the duration of the project. Because the uncertainty of continued employment for those assigned to the project is a significant disadvantage of this form of organization, a third form of organization has emerged. In the *matrix* organization (Figure 10-3), authority

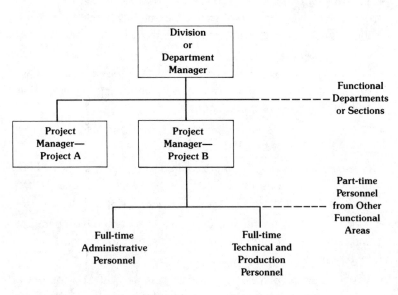

Figure 10-2. A project organization.

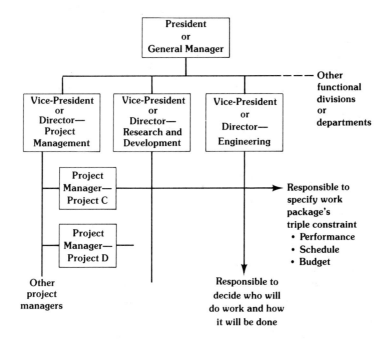

Figure 10-3. A matrix organization.

for the project is clearly established but specialists remain in their functional areas.

The exact nature of the project and matrix organizations may vary over an entire spectrum. At one extreme is the one-person approach. A project manager exercises influence over functional departments with no staff reporting directly to him or her. Another design is the staff approach in which the project manager is provided a staff for cost control, scheduling, change control, and supervision, but the work is carried out by the functional departments. A third approach is the pure matrix form in which some primary tasks are removed from functional departments and assigned directly to the project manager, who also supervises a staff responsible for control and scheduling. The most complex approach is the total aggregate one in which the project manager is in charge of all staff and all departments necessary to complete the project. More specifically, consider the following three options:

- The project manager advises the functional departments as to what results are required. Each departmental manager is a subcontractor who is responsible for a certain result at a particular cost by some point in time. Departmental employees are responsible to their supervisor and do not deal directly with the project manager.

Project and matrix approaches vary

- The project manager directs the personnel who complete the project. He or she designs their work packages, but their department heads choose the team and are responsible for results.

- The project manager is provided equipment and personnel from departments and is responsible for all results and supervision.

Clearly, the basic characteristic that differentiates project or matrix management from functional management is the structuring of roles and authority relationships. Emphasis is upon horizontal and diagonal flows of information and interaction rather than vertical flow of authority. Also, the project or matrix organization is concerned with stringent cost, performance, and schedule constraints for a finite project rather than ongoing repetitive production and sales.

Research has shown that project and matrix approaches have several advantages relative to the functional design:[2]

- Better control of the project.
- Improved customer relations.
- Reduced design and development time.
- Improved quality and reliability.
- Lower costs, thus higher profits.
- Better security.

At times, however, the project approach makes internal operations more complicated, creates conflicts with company policies, and causes tendencies for functional departments to neglect their ongoing tasks.

Top Management Determines Which Approach

Which organizational approach is to be used is determined by the nature of the objectives and the best judgment of top management. Size or complexity alone do not distinguish projects from other activities.[3] The definitive characteristics are *origin* (a one-of-a-kind mission which originates because some important result must be accomplished), *product* (a specified output, which terminates the project), *marketplace* (a specified consumer, usually in some other organization), and *resources* (people and things under the control of other managers).

The basic objective of the project is to produce a product that will satisfy the specifications, within cost and on schedule. The atomic bomb, weapons systems such as Polaris or Minuteman, and the Bay Area Rapid Transit system are examples of such projects. The project or matrix forms may also be beneficial in smaller undertakings such as installation of a new EDP system, marketing a unique product, launching a new advertising campaign, or merging corporations. Four basic criteria help management in deciding whether or not a given program justifies this departure from the functional form:

- *Size.* Is the program larger than previous projects undertaken by the organization? Are there substantially larger sums of money and numbers of people involved?

- *Risk.* Are the potential problems of failure or delay critical to the well-being of the total organization? Are the corresponding penalties severe?

- *Interdependence.* Are the tasks within the project complex and interrelated across the company's functional departments? These relationships among research, development, production, and finance are crucial. Will it be difficult to reconcile problems at these interfaces with the current organization? Does the present organization possess the necessary flexibility and responsiveness?

- *Uniqueness.* Is there sufficient familiarity with the project or does it require knowledge used infrequently? Lack of precedent creates hesitation and disagreement, particularly at lower levels of management. Will these be detrimental in this project?

Criteria management uses to decide which form

If top management gives an affirmative answer to several of these questions, they may consider abandoning the functional form in favor of some superimposed project model. For example, a project which is very large, very risky, highly interdependent, and unique to the organization might be managed with the total aggregate project approach. Installation of a new computer might be managed by a single project manager with a small staff. It is also worth noting that as the project progresses toward completion, the project team may change from one of the above designs to another, depending upon the nature of the project and the relative success in the approach being used at any point in time.

You may be an electrical engineer assigned to a computer design project, or a mechanical engineer working in a materials applications program. Or perhaps you are a civil engineer managing a portion of a construction project. If you are involved in any technical efforts that your top management has decided to "projectize," you should be aware of potential hazards that exist in your current assignment. These potential problems and some specific ways the project manager you report to can deal with them are the subjects of the following two sections.

Some Potential Problems of Project Organization

The project model of organization has been very successful in bringing new products to market faster than competitors, meeting technical commitments at lower cost, and completing major expansions on schedule. Some claim it may be the organization form of the future for large, technology-based firms. Unfortunately, it is far from a cure-all for the inefficiencies, delays, and human problems experienced by even the best-managed organizations. Elimination of managerial problems is not one of its valid claims. Top management, the project manager, and members of the team are likely to experience some unique difficulties as the project is accomplished.

First, consider the problems of team members. Research has shown they suffer more anxieties about loss of employment than functional personnel. When the project is nearing completion, team members become increasingly insecure and frustrated. Predictably, they tend to stretch out the project if another is not readily available. Team members do not know who their boss is and so feel lost without a permanent departmental anchor. "Who should I impress and please in order to be promoted and rewarded?" Team members worry more about being decelerated in their careers because no clear path is apparent.

Members of project teams are subject to uncertainty

For all these reasons team members feel less loyalty to their employer than do functional employees. Also, they are subject to

134

uncertainties about company policy and formal procedures because of inconsistencies in interpretation. Their personal development is often neglected because primary attention is focused upon completion of the project in the short term rather than long-term development of personnel. They will not be working for the project manager when the team is dissolved, so why should he or she spend time and resources on their training and development? Thus, technical employees tend to become progressively specialized and increasingly narrow in their skills.

The project manager must cope with all of these problems as well as a special set of his or her own. He or she is vulnerable to top management errors. Frequently, top executives who are unfamiliar with the project make ill-advised decisions that jeopardize the project. Untimely intervention that undercuts the project manager is common. Sometimes this is out of personal whim, but more often it is caused by lack of awareness and a feeling of lost authority and control. Another problem is caused by authority uncertainties. Who decides? The project manager or the department head? There are always innumerable possibilities for interdepartmental conflict and uncertainty. Superimposed upon this issue of decision authority is the necessity for *fast* decisions. In many projects a delay of a single day can cost hundreds of thousands of dollars, particularly if the project is nearing completion. Someone must move fast but *who*? And in which direction? The most common tradeoffs requiring fast decisions are those involving a reduction in quality in order to save time or cost or those requiring an increase in cost to remain on schedule. There are usually no easy answers.

The project manager also faces uncertainty

In dealing with these problems, the project manager must maintain a careful balance between the technical and managerial functions, must communicate project objectives expertly, and must avoid both technical and managerial obsolescence. One of the saddest statements I have ever heard was made by a friend nearing the end of his project. "I am not yet an experienced manager. Now I am an obsolete engineer to boot; and I am too old to return to school!"

How Well Is Your Project Manager Doing?

At the heart of project management is one person, the project manager, who is responsible for planning, coordination, scheduling,

135

cost control, and the ultimate completion of the program. This manager is usually selected from the ranks of middle management, and you are subject to his authority and control. He or she must possess a good technical background, management skills, and consummate human relations capabilities. He must be able to communicate clearly and, absolutely, must be results oriented. And he must be able to allow personal freedom by permitting others to perform tasks differently than he himself might do them.

If the project team is to be held accountable for successful completion of the program, the project manager and team members (if the manager wishes to delegate some aspects of the project authority) must also be responsible for and have the requisite authority in the following areas:

- *Definition of the objective.* What is the product in terms of performance criteria, quality, reliability, and maintenance? This includes all hardware, software, and service. What are the schedules and cost factors?

- *Customer relations.* The team maintains outside contacts with a constant awareness of customer requirements, attitudes, and future business possibilities beyond the current project.

- *Funds control.* The team must be able to release funding to those departments performing tasks and must have authority to buy goods or services outside the firm if dissatisfied with company sources. They decide the source of supply if outside purchases are necessary.

- *Change control.* They must possess sole authority for changes in design specifications and other project characteristics.

- *Subcontracts.* They control and supervise all subcontractors providing inputs to the project.

The amount of authority delegated to the project manager is critical. Since successful completion depends to a large extent upon support provided by functional groups, the authority, or the lack of it, of the project manager must be spelled out explicitly. Many companies have found this to be simpler than it may seem. If the manager has authority over money, schedules, and performance criteria, then he or she has the "teeth" necessary for completion of the project. The final requirement is the firm backing of top management when problems develop and push comes to shove, which will inevitably happen in every project.

The project manager should design the least complicated team possible, surround him- or herself with the best people possible, and design and utilize formal control mechanisms. Beyond this, the project manager should do all of the following things for maximum success:

- Start with a definite plan, the top spec's in terms of specific results. Communicate this plan to everyone on the team.

- Make managers of subprojects into business partners. Assign them responsibility. Give them authority. Provide the necessary support and funds for completion of assigned tasks. Make certain they are cost, schedule, and performance conscious.

- Use a control system that continuously isolates variances from the plan at two levels, the functional subdivision level for those not under direct control and the task level for subordinate team managers.

- Use a frequent, perhaps weekly, review session to monitor program status. Pay close attention to deviations. Concentrate upon exceptions by allowing subordinates to manage the routine. *Prevent* serious problems rather than trying to solve them later.

- Enforce rigid change control. Any change costs money. A formal revision process must be defined and followed to make certain dollars spent now will in fact save dollars later. Make advocates of design changes *prove* the advantages.

- Recognize the crucial relationship between time and cost. Acceleration of the project costs much less in initial stages. Early acceleration is always preferred to a crash effort in final stages, which usually generates enormous and unjustifiable costs.

- Remember that the eighty/twenty rule applies to every project. Twenty percent of the effort will account for 80 percent of the cost and performance problems. Concentrate on these critical few aspects and assign the best people to them.

A plan for the project manager

The project manager must maintain a careful balance between the managerial and technical aspects of the project. If a development engineer tells the manager that a particular component has a reliability factor less than that called for in the spec's, the manager must weigh this shortfall in technical performance against the managerial aspects of cost and schedule. He cannot overemphasize technical aspects to the detriment of cost and schedule. The tradeoffs

137

here are crucial. The solution is to leave the complicated technical issues to the team (that is what they are there for) and maintain broad controls over schedules and costs. This is difficult for some managers because they possess technical expertise themselves and tend to overly involve themselves in technical details to the detriment of managerial issues.

Also, it is important for project managers to establish and maintain good communications channels with other managers and with workers. The best way to do this is to *circulate and ask*. Too few engineering managers are willing to go out and mingle with the troops. These managers will never know what is really going on. They are asking for trouble, and they will get it!

Even the best project manager will not be able to accomplish project objectives without offending other members of management, perhaps even those managers responsible for his or her promotion and salary increases. This is a fact of life. I recall a parable involving an old man and a boy taking a journey on a donkey. The old man was chastised by a passerby for riding the beast while the boy walked. They switched and were criticized by another traveler. So they both rode the donkey and were roasted by several for cruelty to a dumb animal. At this point, the old man tied the donkey's legs together and inserted a long pole so that he and the boy could carry the beast. While crossing a river, the old man slipped and the donkey fell into the water and, because his legs were tied, he drowned. The moral of the story is worth remembering for all managers:

Try to please everybody and you will end up losing your ass.

Summary

- The functional model of organization is usually not effective in accomplishment of one-time, complicated missions.
- The project and matrix forms of organization are advantageous in management of these complicated, unique missions.
- Four criteria top management may use in deciding whether or not to use the project or matrix form are size, risk, interdependence, and uniqueness.

- Problems are caused for team members and the project manager by insecurity, uncertain authority, and top management errors.
- The project manager is the key. He or she must define results, concentrate on variances in important functions, enforce rigid change control, analyze tradeoffs intelligently, and circulate and ask.

Notes

1. Figures 10-1, 2, 3 are taken from M. D. Rosenau, Jr., *Successful Project Management* (Belmont, Calif.: Lifetime Learning Publications, 1981). This is an excellent work that provides a step-by-step approach to project management with many practical examples and an experienced, real world flavor.

2. See C. J. Middleton, "How to Set Up a Project Organization," *Harvard Business Review* (March–April 1967), p. 73.

3. This idea is expressed by Rosenau, in *Successful Project Management*.

Further Readings

1. Several worthwhile articles dealing with the problems of project management are:
   A. G. Butler, Jr., "Project Management: A Study in Organizational Conflict," *Academy of Management Journal* (March 1975), p. 84; J. R. Gunderman and F. W. McMurry, "Making Project Management Work," *Journal of Systems Management* (February 1975), p. 426; C. Reeser, "Some Potential Human Problems in the Project Form of Organization," *Academy of Management Journal* (December 1969), p. 459.

2. In addition to the Rosenau work cited above, three texts dealing with project management are:
   C. C. Martin, *Project Management: How to Make It Work* (New York: AMACOM, 1976); J. A. Morton, *Organization for Innovation* (New York: McGraw-Hill, 1971); J. D. Wiest and F. K. Levy, *A Management Guide to PERT/CPM* (Englewood Cliffs, N.J.: Prentice-Hall, 1969).

11.

Understanding Strategy

I have often tried to set down the strategic truths I have comprehended in the form of simple anecdotes, and they rank this way in my mind. One of them is the celebrated tale of the hunter who gave powdered poison to a bear. He mixed the powder with the greatest care, making sure that not only the ingredients but the proportions were absolutely correct. He rolled it up in a large paper, and was about to blow it down the bear's throat. But the bear blew first.

WINSTON S. CHURCHILL

From this chapter you will learn:

- *Why you, as a new manager, should be concerned about strategy*
- *What the difference is between strategy and tactics, and why both are important*
- *How strategy is set*
- *Why strategy must allow for growth, and how strategy should change as an organization grows*

If you were designing an oil refinery you would not start by designing or assembling a heat exchanger, would you? Nor would you start the design of a major jet aircraft by specifying the nature of the landing gear. The overall dimensions, weight, and performance characteristics must be established before the subsystems are designed, if they are to function effectively. This principle also holds for the management of a firm and the technical subsystems of that firm. Top management must take an overall, long-range, global look . . . a searching, intelligent look within, a critical look around, and a long look ahead. Then major goals and objectives can be specified and the functional plans, policies, and organizational structure necessary to achieve these goals can be defined. All of this must relate to changing environment, resources, and values.

As a new technical manager, you should be aware of the importance of your top management's strategy, or else the definition and accomplishment of specific short-run objectives will make no sense to you. Furthermore, if you wish to maximize your chances of making it to top management you must begin *now* to think about strategy and how your organizational unit relates to the long-term objectives of your firm. The purpose of this chapter is to introduce you to strategic thinking and give you a basic awareness of its importance.

What Is Strategy, and Why Is It Important?

Corporate strategy begins with the questions, "What are we in business for?" and "Where are we headed?" It is a concerted effort to give the firm a chance at influencing its destiny as against going along with the luck of the draw. Strategic planning is initiated at the top of the organization by boards of directors, presidents, and chief operating executives.

Strategy is global and starts at the top

In military terms, strategy is a matter of large-scale campaigns and total war carried out by armies and entire branches of armed services under the command of flag rank officers and the commander-in-chief. Tactics, on the other hand, is a matter of single engagements and the techniques used to overcome the enemy in that battle. Tactical forces would include smaller units up to divisions or numbered air forces under the command of line officers. The concepts of military and corporate tactics and strategy are directly analogous.

If an organization does not have an intelligent strategy, then no matter how well tactics are handled, the organization will fail. For example, I worked for General Dynamics when it was competing directly against Boeing and Douglas in design, construction, and marketing of jet passenger aircraft. Boeing had an edge because the U.S. Government had paid for the development of the KC-135 jet tanker, which with minor modifications became the 707 airliner. Douglas had an edge because it had started design of the DC-8 years earlier. Rather than concede this market to two capable competitors who already had an advantage, the top management of my firm decided to compete directly with them for the long-range aircraft market by differentiating their product vis-a-vis the 707 and the DC-8. This strategy was ill-founded as it was based on trying to recoup losses on a poor initial decision, unwillingness to make a tough choice, and considerations of corporate image and male ego. It yielded disaster for my firm. When the chief of cost estimation informed top management that the incremental cost of each aircraft (the cost of purchased components, engines, direct material, and direct labor) was several hundred thousand dollars more than the selling price (which meant that out of this negative margin we had to pay for administrative overhead and profit), he was fired. Top management did not believe him and so they increased marketing efforts. "Lose a little on each aircraft but make it up in volume." As you might expect, the final result was a loss of several hundred million dollars.

You cannot blame this loss on poor tactics except perhaps the firing of the chief of cost estimation. The strategy was to blame. Macro decisions committed a significant portion of the firm's resources to head-to-head competition with a pair of capable competitors who started with critical advantages. It is interesting to speculate about what the current status of Convair would be if the strategy had been to develop a medium-range 727 type of design or a short-range 737 type, conceding the long-range market to Boeing and Douglas. Instead, an abysmal strategy committed the firm to a no-win situation, the result being a well-run near-bankruptcy. The moral of this story is that *bad strategy overwhelms good tactics.*

Superb tactics cannot overcome inept strategy

What Are Tactics and Why Are They Important?

As a lower-level technical manager you are likely to be involved with carrying out tactics concerned with short-term levels of production, quality control, product design, or other similar functions. Tactics are activities which implement strategy; they are critical in providing stability and control over the immediate future.

In the same way that bad strategy overwhelms good tactics, bad tactics can prevent accomplishment of competent strategy. You may recall that the first successful electronic digital computer was developed by two scientists at the University of Pennsylvania. The Electronic Numerical Integrator and Computer (ENIAC) was a thirty-ton, one-hundred-fifty-kilowatt monster that used vacuum tubes and manipulated discrete numbers rather than continuous analogs. Shortly after World War II, the developers of this computer and its immediate progeny sold the resulting UNIVAC organization to Remington Rand. This corporation completely integrated the UNIVAC Division, which meant that identical marketing tactics were used for all product lines. For example, no computers were made for stock: first an order had to be received, and then a computer was built to satisfy that order. This tactical blunder limited growth and allowed a small unknown competitor named International Business Machines to awaken and mature. We all know what the end result has been. The opportunity losses in terms of foregone profits suffered since by UNIVAC dwarf the losses sustained by the Convair Division of General Dynamics.

Inept tactics can overwhelm competent strategy

How Strategy Is Set

Obviously, a successful organization must have an intelligent strategy as well as effective tactics. If the firm is to survive and prosper, strategic objectives must be well thought out, beginning with definition of financial objectives in terms of long-term return to shareholders. Other relevant objectives are then defined that are consistent with this return.

In setting strategy, top management must concentrate upon certain questions and their answers:

The key strategic questions

- Where are we now in the critical dimensions of our organization? What business are we really in? What are our strengths? Our weaknesses? Where are the threats? The opportunities?
- Where do we want to be in, say, three to five years?
- Are we growing too much? Too little? About right?
- How is our management group? Our technical people?

144

- What are the trends? Where are we headed? If we keep doing things as we are now, where will we be in three to five years?
- Are obstacles developing that will prevent us from being where we want to be in five years? What can we do about these now?

The time frame of these questions is long-term and the focus is macro or global. Answers to these questions deal with terms such as *return on investment, earnings per share, diversification, risk, competitive advantage, environmental trends, market share,* etc.

Production, research, financial, and marketing plans are then generated and subjected to a long-term analysis. The final product of this analysis is a long-term plan that matches opportunity and capability at a tolerable level of risk. *Then* tactics are devised to achieve these plans.

As an example of how the strategy-setting process works, consider this list of current trends in the business environment that might be generated:

1. More environmental protection legislation and enforcement (air, water, etc.).
2. Increased competition from worldwide sources.
3. More governmental controls in domestic affairs (other than the environment).
4. Increased international competition for raw materials.
5. Higher raw material and labor prices.
6. Lower levels of increase in productivity by U.S. labor.
7. More pressure for social reforms.
8. Freer world trade with trends toward specialization in some countries.
9. Increased transportation costs.
10. Unionization of heretofore nonunionized workforces.

Some strategic trends in our environment

This list is not exhaustive, of course, and the items are not independent of each other. Energy is a raw material of sorts and increased competition for it is a factor in driving up costs of operation, including transportation.

It is important for top management to recognize that these trends exist but that is not sufficient. How will they affect the firm? The function of management? How can a plan be devised now to minimize the impact of these trends or, better yet, use them to the firm's competitive advantage? For example, stone, glass, clay, and primary metal industries consume the most energy as a percentage of the total cost of their production. Food and lumber industries consume intermediate amounts. Tobacco and printing consume the least. The energy crisis will have considerably different impacts upon firms in these various industries. This fact must be a component of their strategies for success (or perhaps survival) in the next decade.

Trends affect
firms
differently

Strategy Must Allow for Controlled Growth

Any effective strategy must deal with growth. If a firm is not growth-oriented it is difficult to attract and retain competent employees. It becomes prey for the competition. Innovation and vitality die. The literature is full of tales of organizations that stagnated and in many cases perished. Montgomery Ward immediately comes to mind. Their no-growth philosophy and its ultimate effect on sales and profits is a graphic illustration of the basic principle that *a firm must grow to remain viable. It cannot stand still.* But this growth must be carefully managed and, to do this, it must be understood.

Growth is
necessary for
survival

Considerable research has shown that growth patterns of most organizations from simple origins to complex levels of development have very definite characteristics. The dynamic growth of businesses, national economies, mass movements, government agencies, labor unions, and even fruit flies in a confined environment, exhibit similar stages of growth.

The common pattern of the growth process over time is shown in Figure 11-1. The first phase begins at the origin when an entrepreneur establishes the firm. Size is small and, for relatively long periods of time, growth is slow. The second phase is characterized by accelerated growth and significant, rapid increases in size. The third phase is one of maturation and complexity.

I prefer to call the first phase the *Wonder* stage of the firm. The entrepreneur says "I wonder if it will work. I wonder if we can survive. I wonder if we should have tried this at all!" When phase one ends, disequilibrium has occurred for any of a number of reasons and growth accelerates abruptly. This is the *Thunder* phase.

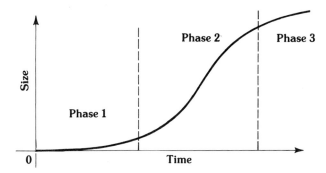

Figure 11-1. The typical pattern of growth over time.

Not only is the firm increasing in size but the rate of increase is increasing. Eventually, a point of inflection is reached during phase two. The firm is still increasing in size but the rate of growth is decreasing. This commences the *Plunder* phase. Phase three is somewhat more difficult to describe. Initially, it might be described as the *Slumber* phase. If the organization is a governmental agency or a university, the size levels off with sustained minor growth or decline and the organization remains indefinitely in the Slumber mode with an assured source of revenue. Business firms, however, often switch in phase three to the *Blunder* stage, followed soon after by *Under*.

The life cycle of a typical U.S. corporation . . . Wonder, Thunder, Plunder, Slumber, Blunder, Under

As an example of this model, consider the case of the Pepsi-Cola Company. A pharmacist named Caleb D. Bradham developed a product, "Brad's Drink," in New Bern, North Carolina. In 1898, young Caleb gave his drink the name "Pepsi-Cola." In 1902, Bradham turned over the management of his drugstore to his uncle so he could concentrate upon the marketing of his drink. Thus began the Wonder phase. Growth was slight and it was three years before Bradham moved into his own building and began to establish franchises in other locations. The number of franchises is shown in Figure 11-2 as a function of time. In 1911, three hundred bottlers were franchised to market Pepsi and the Thunder and Plunder phases were nearly complete. The maximum number of Pepsi bottlers franchised by Bradham is not known; however, the rapid

147

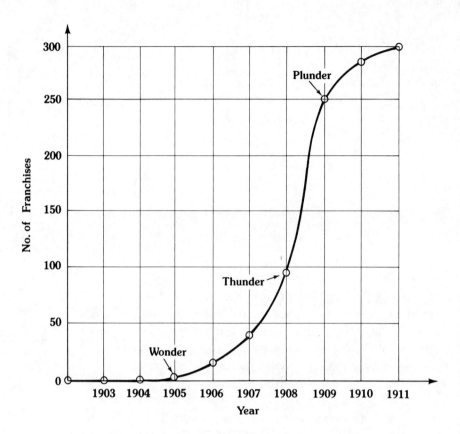

Figure 11-2. Initial stages in the life cycle of the Pepsi-Cola Company.

growth of the 1907–10 period subsided. By 1915 the product was sold in at least twenty-four states. Bradham was well known, wealthy, and mentioned as a candidate for governor. At forty-eight years of age he was heavily involved with the daily operation of his firm and its growing pains. There was no doubt in his firm as to who made the decisions.

Then World War I hit and the world market for sugar, a critical ingredient of Pepsi, was profoundly changed. The wartime price of 5½¢ per pound increased to 22½¢ by 1920. With no apparent long-term strategy concerning the acquisition of sugar and struggling to manage his now complex organization, Bradham made a mistake. He bought sugar heavily at 22½¢ and within months the price dropped to about 3¢. Bradham's working capital was gone. To cover sizable losses, he borrowed money and sold assets but could not raise enough capital from these sources. Common and preferred shares were offered but no one bought. By early 1922 the company was insolvent and by March 1923 the company was bankrupt. Its assets were sold to pay creditors and Bradham was broken.

The Wonder, Thunder, Plunder, Slumber, Blunder, and Under cycle took about twenty years. The resurrected organization now known as Pepsico was built by others. It has current sales in excess of two billion dollars per year but Caleb Bradham died bankrupt. In Bradham's case, a tactical error that resulted from a lack of sound strategy was the blunder that took him under.

In some cases, it is uncontrolled growth that takes firms under. Consider a product called "Weedone," a chemical formulation used to kill common lawn weeds. A week after application the average homeowner thinks a terrible mistake has been made. The grass looks the same but the weeds are lush and twice as large as when Weedone was applied. "Did I *fertilize* the weeds?" Two weeks later the weeds are larger but showing signs of difficulty. In another week they are dead! They have literally grown themselves to death. Weedone stimulates the weeds to grow so rapidly that they outgrow their sources of nourishment and starve. Also, their internal systems are not able to deal with such rapid increases in size and complexity. The same is true for a business organization.

It is possible for a firm to grow so fast it outstrips its resources (management, working capital, production and research capability) and grows itself to death!

A firm can grow itself to death

W. T. Grant and Boise Cascade are vivid examples of the truth of this principle. A good strategy should not allow this to happen.

Strategy Must Change as Growth Occurs

So now we know that planning for growth is an important component of strategy and we know that no growth or too much growth can both be fatal. What can we infer about how strategy and tactics must change if an organization is to survive growth?

Assume you are the captain of a small naval vessel, say, a U.S. Navy Fast Patrol Craft. This craft has two diesels and a crew of eleven including two junior officers. The length of the vessel is about ninety feet. As the captain you can stand on the bridge and see from bow to stern. You know each member of the crew. The range of the craft is limited and the missions are fairly straightforward. In this situation, who makes the decisions? *You do!* You can fire off decisions concerning the engines, the radio, the navigation, and offensive or defensive tactics, because the ship is small and maneuverable enough so that you can get away with centralization of authority except for regular duties routinely carried out by the other officers and crew.

Let's keep you in the Navy but place you instead on the bridge of the U.S.S. Enterprise, a Nimitz-class nuclear carrier. You have command of a vessel with a length in excess of eleven hundred feet, a crew of almost five thousand (including 425 officers), and a very complex nuclear power plant. Your missions are complex and your hardware is awesome, including nuclear capability. You cannot see from bow to stern and your vessel is not very maneuverable. In this situation, who makes the decisions? *Not you!* Or rather, you make the strategic decisions and deal with exceptions to the routine while your officers manage the ship. One officer is in charge of the signal bridge, another in charge of the engine rooms, another in charge of the radio room, etc. These are highly trained, competent officers who know what is expected of them in terms of performance. They know what decisions they can make and which ones must be made by the Captain. If you are to survive as the commanding officer of the Enterprise you must use well-designed *decentralization* of authority. It is physically impossible to run your ship any other way.

Obviously, this analogy is valid for other organizations. A small business firm is analogous to the patrol craft. Still in the Wonder phase, there is a general absence of formal objectives and well-defined structure. The objective is comfort and survival over the short term, the success and well-being of the owner and perhaps a few top executives. Power is concentrated at the top. Decisions are often conservative and short term in nature. Policies are unwritten. Growth is unplanned. The chief operating executive can see from bow to stern. Communication is informal.

As this firm enters the Thunder and Plunder stages, some notable changes occur. The management group grows in size and becomes more heterogeneous. Optimism pervades but the need for written policies becomes more apparent. Centralized authority becomes strained as the momentum of the growth carries the firm onward and upward. Then, as growth begins to subside, the need for controls, plans, and communication is obvious.

This is a critical time for the organization. It is approaching the Enterprise size and requires a more professional, rational management group. Obviously, not all firms complete the cycle through Slumber, Blunder, and Under. There are numerous large, successful organizations that were small and maneuverable at one time and then survived rapid growth. Their strategies likely accommodated the following changes that are inevitable if a firm is to grow successfully:

Firms change as they grow and strategy must change too

- *As a firm grows, the nature of the administrators has to change or different administrators must be found.* Large, complex organizations require different types of managers than do small firms.

- A *transition must be made from informal planning and decision making to rational, professional techniques.* The techniques that made the firm big will not be successful when it becomes big! Decisions must be made carefully. Results must be emphasized. Expectations must be known. A long-term strategy must be defined.

- *As the top management group grows in size, it must be concerned with the total firm and long-term survival.* Middle and lower management must be left alone to run the firm from day to day, week to week.

- *Authority must become decentralized.* Authority for making all the decisions, once concentrated at the top, must come to rest with middle and lower management except for certain, specific areas of concern that are reserved for top management.

The stages of growth discussed above apply to *parts* of firms as well as to firms as a whole. For example, an entrepreneur may start a company in order to market a single invention. As the company grows, innovation and disequilibrium occur. The firm is suddenly larger by an order of magnitude. There is now a need for a professional research and development group. An R&D director is appointed, special facilities built or set aside, and so on. This part of the company is now entering the Wonder phase although the firm

Parts of the organization also go through stages of growth

151

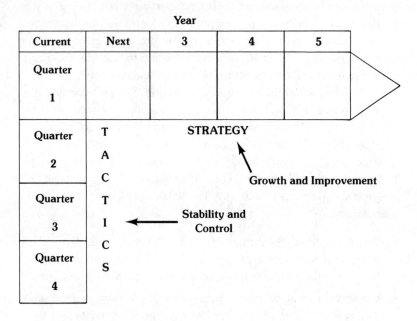

Figure 11-3. How tactics and strategy work together.

itself may be in the advanced portion of the Plunder phase. Thus, all of the generalizations made above now apply to the R&D group and it will survive only if the growth transitions are managed skill-fully, with a strategy that expects growth and that stretches to ac-commodate it.

How Tactics and Strategy Work Together

A firm's strategic plan looks out over the horizon for, say, five years. It is adjusted annually by dropping the previous year off and adding another year on the end. As shown in Figure 11-3, strategy concerns itself with long-term growth and improvement with the setting of yearly and five-year objectives, while tactics relate to quarterly objectives defined so that top management may track progress of the organization according to the long-term game plan.

Ideally, the tactical short-term objectives are the responsibility of middle and lower management. If these are tied directly to the long-term strategy, as they should be, and if they are defined in terms of results so that expectations are known, then top management is assured of short-term stability and control. Or, as a minimum, if the firm or one area of the firm begins to get out of control, that fact will be known before it is fatal.

Tactics assure stability and control; strategy assures growth and improvement

Now it is obvious where you as a technical manager fit into the entire picture. Your objectives are most likely tactical in nature and oriented toward stability and control. You are running the ship and helping it remain afloat as it grows over time. Perhaps you are also charged with sealing some leaky areas and improving the climate for other members of the crew.

If you are a new technical manager involved in R&D, know that the foundation of any successful research and development effort, especially that portion dealing with new product development, is long-term strategy. As Milton Rosenau states, "You must know both where the new product development effort is expected to take the company and how the company will get there or you have no rationale for choosing new products to develop."[1] Long-term growth and survival of the firm require profitable new and redesigned products. It is rare that the present product line of a firm can generate stable, long-term growth. Income from present products will gradually decline. This reduction as well as growth in sales must come from improved present products as well as new ones. Thus, if research and new product development are to be successful, they must be meshed with and integrated into an intelligent long-term strategy.

Summary

- Strategy is a long-term global plan concerned with the current status of the organization, where it is trending, and what can be done now in macro terms to maximize the probability it will be where it should be in, say, five years.
- Superb tactics cannot overcome inept strategy. Stupid tactics can ruin competent strategy. Both must be done well.

- An important aspect of strategy is the proper management of growth. No growth or too much growth are both undesirable. Growth must be persistent but in control.
- Lower and middle managers are primarily concerned with tactics (stability and control). The concept of strategy becomes more important as one rises to higher levels in the organization.
- The foundation of successful research and development is competent strategy.

Note

1. See M. D. Rosenau, Jr., *Innovation: Managing the Development of Profitable New Products* (Belmont, Calif.: Lifetime Learning Publications, 1982), p. 3.

Further Readings

1. W. F. Christopher, *Management for the 1980's* (Englewood Cliffs, N.J.: Prentice-Hall, 1980). This paperback book is written by an experienced manager and is addressed to the special problems that will confront the manager in this decade. Chapters 3 through 6 deal with defining identity, setting goals, the strategy compass, and the organization's mission.

2. R. G. Murdick, R. H. Eckhouse, and R. C. Moor, *Business Policy: A Framework for Analysis* (Columbus, Ohio: Grid Publishing, 1980). This paperback work shows how to diagnose a firm that is potentially in trouble. The analysis required to design a specific, strategic plan of action is outlined. Separate chapters deal with the functional areas of marketing, finance, production, engineering, R&D, etc.

3. W. H. Newman and J. P. Logan, *Strategy, Policy and Central Management*, Eighth Edition (Cincinnati: South-Western Publishing, 1981). This work emphasizes the operational aspects that make strategy work by linking the formulation of long-range objectives with workable short-term courses of action. The book is built around a model for sorting out major pieces of the total picture and relating these pieces to each other.

4. B. Tregoe and J. Zimmerman, *Top Management Strategy: What It Is and How to Make It Work* (New York: Simon & Schuster, 1980). This short book argues that every business has a "driving force" that is the center of important activities. How this force operates and how to set strategic goals around it are the primary messages of the work.

12.

Managing Your Career

*Destiny is not a matter of chance, it is a matter of choice;
it is not a thing to be waited for, it is a thing to be
achieved.*

WILLIAM J. BRYAN

From this chapter you will learn:

- *Why management of your time is important to your success, and how you can do it better*
- *Where you are in your career life cycle*
- *What you can do to help yourself and your career grow*
- *Why you should be prepared for frustration to accompany your increased knowledge*

Just as you have a responsibility to help your subordinates grow and develop, you also have a responsibility to manage your own career, to the extent that it is possible. You do not merely have a job. You have a career. It can be managed competently or it can be ignored. Much of the responsibility for this rests squarely on your shoulders.

This chapter begins with a discussion of time management, since time is an important raw material of your career. We will also look at the career life cycle and at some specific ways you can enhance your own career progress.

Making the Most of Your Time

As a new manager you will soon find you have many more demands upon your time than time available to allocate to these demands. Now is the stage of your career to develop habits that will promote your success and help you avoid a coronary. You must develop a strategy to utilize your time effectively. It is one of your scarcest resources. And you cannot save it like most other resources and then use it some other day. You must manage it intelligently, or else work harder and longer hours or get out of management.

If you don't know the value of time you will not be successful in management.

The first step in designing your strategy is to recognize that in order to save and manage time you must know where you are losing it. Research has shown the following to be the most common time wasters:

Identify ways you may be wasting time

- Lack of objectives in terms of results . . . the activity trap.
- Too much effort on the trivial many activities that produce only a small portion of output.
- Management by crisis . . . fighting fires rather than anticipating and preventing them.
- Procrastination . . . postponing unpleasant issues thus allowing them time to become emergencies.
- Interruptions . . . subordinates constantly checking back to clarify instructions, obtain feedback, or have you solve their problems for them.
- Doing "functional" duties . . . routine, recurring activities that can and should be delegated to someone else.
- Meetings . . . unorganized, drifting, vague discussions that conclude with the scheduling of another meeting.
- Paperwork . . . providing numbers or opinions that no one uses for decision making.
- Lack of an alert, conscious plan for managing one's time.

Recognizing these bottomless pits of time-wasting is part of the solution to the problem. The rest of the solution involves some funda-mental principles that you must learn to apply:

- *Concentrate on results.* If the time spent on an activity has no payoff in terms of output, don't do it! Constantly ask yourself the question, "If I don't do this, what will be the consequence?"

- *Identify critical areas.* What is really important? Which are the critical few that generate most of my output? Set priorities.

- *Set target dates for completion of results.* Be relatively optimistic. Recall Parkinson's First Law, "Work expands so as to fill the time available for its completion."

- *Do unpleasant things before they become crises.* Do not put it off if you can do it now and get it out of the way.

- *Learn to delegate.* Give away pieces of your job. Use the excep-tion principle, saving nonroutine decisions and activities for your-self. Don't underestimate the potential of your secretary in this regard.

- *Refuse to solve subordinates' problems.* Support and trust them. Tolerate mistakes when made and turn them into learning experiences.

- *Cut down on paperwork, when within your control.* Don't add a new form unless you discontinue an old one.

- *Develop a sense of urgency in meetings.* Keep control of the dis-cussion and don't convene the meeting unless it is obviously nec-essary. Make sure people are aware of the purpose of the meeting so they can prepare.

Some fundamental principles of time management

If you are able to practice the above principles, you will have taken a giant step toward improving your effectiveness as a manager.

Where Are You in Your Career Life Cycle?

Different phases exist in almost everyone's career:[1]

Age 15 to 23: Establish independence and pull up roots
Age 24 to 29: Early adulthood and initial development of
a professional career

Age 30 to 32: Transition years with reassessment of career and shifting of jobs

Age 33 to 39: Stability and settling down

Age 40 to 45: Mid-life crisis and self-reflection

Age 45 to 55: Restabilization and blossoming

Your approach to career development will depend to a large extent on which of these phases you are in. As discussed in Chapter 7, the problems of a new graduate are different from those of a mid-career manager.

How to Enhance Your Career Progress

Certain principles of career development apply to all managers:

- *Master your current job and train a replacement.* This increases your mobility and will make you stand out as someone who can handle more responsibility.

- *Determine the expectations of your boss in terms of results and concentrate upon achieving these results.* Do not allow yourself to be trapped by activity or by uncertainty concerning what must be accomplished in order to be successful in your job.

- *Seek positions of high visibility.* If you are able to handle visibility and do not want anonymity, do not allow yourself to be lost in low exposure dead-end staff jobs. Do not allow yourself to be trapped under a boss who has not been promoted for, say, the last five years.

- *Continue to grow.* Actively seek experiences and assignments that will stretch your abilities. If you do not have a superior who encourages this, set ambitious goals for yourself and then attain these goals. Make certain you set objectives that, when achieved, will be meaningful to you and make you see yourself as a more competent person.

Move upward by applying these principles

- *If you change jobs or employers, do not ever move laterally, unless you have no choice.* Every new assignment should involve more responsibility, more power, and more challenge.

- *If you are a younger manager, find someone to be your mentor.* Locate someone in the organization whom you respect, who is competent, and who is mobile. Do everything you can to go to work for that person. Then do everything you can to make that person look good. Do not attempt to make yourself look good. Make *him or her* look good. If you really respect him or her, this is not phony. You will be surrounded by people trying to make themselves look good. Make your boss look good and you will stand out in the organization as a unique individual. Then hang on — as your boss moves up, you'll move up.

- *Do not, under any circumstances, no matter how justified, criticize your boss.* If you have a problem with your superior, you may be able to solve it with a face-to-face discussion. If done sensitively, this is effective. But do *not* tell others in the organization about the boss's incompetence. It will always filter back and will hurt you more than anyone else. This is particularly true of your boss's boss. Don't criticize him to his superior, even if it is clearly justified. Keep your mouth shut. If you cannot say anything good, then do not say anything. Or, alternatively, resign and then you can say anything you wish.

Expect Frustration as You Grow

An ancient Chinese philosopher, Lao-Tse, observed that "The farther one pursues knowledge, the less one knows." You have probably observed that this apparent paradox is true. The most knowledgeable individuals often perceive themselves to be the most ignorant.

To understand why this contradiction is true, consider the rectangle shown in Figure 12-1 to represent all knowledge in the world on a particular subject. A single individual knows something about that subject. This is represented by the circle within the rectangle. The interface between what he knows and what knowledge is available (the circumference of the circle) is his perceived ignorance. He perceives that there does exist something about that subject he does not yet know.

Suppose through strong efforts to grow and expand his knowledge he learns more about the subject and his circle of knowledge increases in area. It also increases in circumference! He knows more now but perceives a greater ignorance! For example, before taking a class in statistical inference, one's perceived ignorance concerning

161

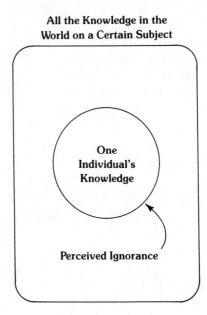

All the Knowledge in the World on a Certain Subject

One Individual's Knowledge

Perceived Ignorance

Figure 12-1. The relationship between knowledge and ignorance.

discriminant analysis or stepwise multiple regression is totally absent. How can you perceive ignorance about a topic when you do not know it exists? After completion of an elementary course in which these topics are mentioned but not dealt with in detail, the individual now perceives the existence of topics about which he knows very little. He is more knowledgeable, perceives he is more ignorant, and is probably more frustrated about the whole thing.

As a manager you must recognize this apparent contradiction in terms and its accompanying frustrations. It applies to you as well as your subordinates. The only person with no perceived ignorance and no resulting frustrations is the one with no knowledge. The subset is empty and, hence, has no area and no circumference. As you master the management skills described in this book, your perceived ignorance may increase. Recognize this frustration as a sign of growth, and resolve to continue to roll back the boundaries of your skills and knowledge.

Perceived ignorance increases with knowledge

162

Summary

- To make the most of your time, identify ways you may be wasting it, and then design a strategy that concentrates on results and eliminates unnecessary activity.
- Recognize that your approach to career development depends upon where you are in your career life cycle.
- Master your job, achieve expected results, continue to grow, locate a mentor, avoid criticizing your boss, and you will rise in your organization.
- Knowledge and perceived ignorance increase together. Thus, personal growth causes frustration. Be prepared for it.

Note

1. Adapted from R. A. Webber, *Management: Basic Elements of Managing Organizations*, revised ed. (Homewood, Ill.: Richard D. Irwin, 1979), p. 544.

Further Readings

1. An informative work that should be read by every new and aspiring manager is G. Bowman, "What Helps or Harms Promotability?" *Harvard Business Review* (May–June 1964), p. 184.
2. A logical next step in your development as a manager might be for you to read W. C. Giegold, *Practical Management Skills for Engineers and Scientists* (Belmont, Calif.: Lifetime Learning Publications, 1982). This book covers in greater detail the management skills introduced here.
3. For a practical and thorough discussion of career planning geared toward technical professionals, see T. Schmidt, *Managing Your Career Success* (Belmont, Calif.: Lifetime Learning Publications, 1982).
4. An excellent work on stages in one's life is G. Sheehy, *Passages: Predictable Crises of Adult Life* (New York: Dutton, 1976).

Index